the
successful
candidate

PEARSON
Prentice Hall
BUSINESS

Books that make you better

Books that make you better. That make you *be* better, *do* better, *feel* better. Whether you want to upgrade your personal skills or change your job, whether you want to improve your managerial style, become a more powerful communicator, or be stimulated and inspired as you work.

Prentice Hall Business is leading the field with a new breed of skills, careers and development books. Books that are a cut above the mainstream – in topic, content and delivery – with an edge and verve that will make you better, with less effort.

Books that are as sharp and smart as you are.

Prentice Hall Business.
We work harder – so you don't have to.

For more details on products, and to contact us, visit
www.pearsoned.co.uk
www.yourmomentum.com

the successful candidate

how to be the person they want to hire

ROS JAY

London • New York • Toronto • Sydney • Tokyo • Singapore
Hong Kong • Cape Town • Madrid • Paris • Amsterdam • Munich • Milan

PEARSON EDUCATION LIMITED

Head Office:
Edinburgh Gate
Harlow CM20 2JE
Tel: +44 (0)1279 623623
Fax: +44 (0)1279 431059
Websites: www.pearsoned.co.uk

_____

First published in Great Britain in 2004

© Pearson Education Limited 2004

The right of Ros Jay to be identified as author of this work has been asserted
by her in accordance with the Copyright, Designs and Patents Act 1988.

ISBN 0 273 67522 2

British Library Cataloguing in Publication Data
A CIP catalogue record for this book can be obtained from the British Library

10 9 8 7 6 5 4 3 2 1

Typeset by Northern Phototypesetting Co. Ltd, Bolton
Printed and bound in Great Britain by Bell & Bain Ltd, Glasgow

The Publishers' policy is to use paper manufactured from sustainable forests.

Contents

PART IV
Work style 119

PART V
Customer relations 169

About the author

Ros Jay is a freelance writer and a senior associate of the Institute of Direct Marketing. She specializes in marketing communication and management-related subjects. She writes and edits corporate magazines both in print and online.

Ros has written many books, including the bestselling *Fast Thinking Managers Manual, How to Manage Your Boss, How to Get a Pay Rise, Brilliant Interview* and *How to Build a Great Team*. All are published by Prentice Hall Business.

Introduction

You're looking for a job. And it can be a confusing business. Ad after ad says 'the successful candidate will have. . .' or 'the successful candidate will be. . .' followed by a list of qualities or abilities from *pragmatic* to *dynamic, able to initiate change* to *a natural leader*.

But what does it all mean? What does the employer's choice of words say about the job on offer and the kind of person they're looking for? Once you've worked out what they're looking for, how do you show them you've got it? You need to transmit your suitability for the job in your application and CV as well as at interview.

This book is your guide to what all the most used words and phrases in recruitment ads really mean. Before going into all the individual words and phrases, however, here's a brief general guide to making the most of the advice you'll find in this book.

Going for the job

So what do you do when you find a job you want to apply for? Obviously you need to follow the instructions in the ad for how to apply, and get an application form to fill in. Then it's time to settle down and assemble your application.

The first thing to remember is that the purpose of the application is *not* to get you the job. No, you didn't misread that. You're not trying to get the job. So what are you doing? That's simple: you're trying to get an interview.

You want to be interviewed because that's your chance to shine, to show how enthusiastic you can be, how well you come across in person. It's your opportunity to counter any concerns the employer might have. And it's your chance to see what *you* think of *them*. All you want to do at this stage is clinch the interview. So you don't have to prove you can do the job better than any other candidate, which is lucky because there's plenty you really can't prove on paper. You only have to prove that you *might* be the best candidate. That will be enough to get you shortlisted.

Your CV and application

The next point at this stage in your campaign to land your dream job is that your CV won't do as it is. It needs to be improved. How do I know that when I've never seen it? I know it because everyone's CV needs to be improved with every new job they go for.

You improve your CV by customizing it to suit the particular job you're applying for. That means adapting it so that you answer all those specific requirements which the employer has stipulated in the job ad. You'll find plenty of tips throughout this book for ways to adapt your CV according to what the employer is looking for.

You'll find plenty of suggestions in the book to highlight certain points on your CV. In general, your CV should not only list what jobs you've done, but also what your responsibilities were. This is where you make sure that you list anything this particular employer is going to be interested in, and put it near the beginning of the list. So if you're listing a job as a sales executive, for example, your CV might read:

- *August 1999 – October 2000: ABC Company, Sales Executive. Responsibilities included: answering incoming sales calls, advising callers on the range of products and the prices, answering queries and taking orders. Also dealing with queries arising from existing orders and non-deliveries.*

If the job you're applying for specifies someone warm and friendly, you can add *making customers feel welcome* to this list, or *providing a friendly image to customers.*

It's a matter of showing what you've done in the most relevant possible light. Pick out the most important things to mention. For example, if you're applying for a job where you need to be able to communicate in Spanish you should give your Spanish GCSE or A level result (assuming it was decent) even if you don't give all your exam results.

Having said all that, there's no point trying to make out you're something you're not. Certainly you should highlight the best and most relevant skills and experience, but don't fabricate anything. For one thing, it's dishonest. For another, if you get caught it simply isn't worth it; you're almost guaranteed to lose the job simply for your dishonesty.

If you really aren't suited to the job, are you sure you actually want it? Would you be happy in a job where you couldn't perform as well as you could elsewhere? And if you believe you *are* suited to it, even without all the qualifications or experience they're asking for, a broad-minded employer may well still give you that interview you need to show them what you're really made of. Just make sure there's enough on your

CV to tempt them to shortlist you despite a few shortcomings.

Bear in mind, too, that many ads ask for someone who is 'capable of' or 'able to' do a certain thing, such as 'able to manage change'. This doesn't mean you must actually have done it before; merely that you must be able to show that you *could* do it if required. So a CV which doesn't match the requirements perfectly doesn't mean your application is a waste of time. If *you* know you could do the job, just make sure that confidence comes across in your application.

The covering letter

Once you've filled out the application and fine-tuned your CV, you can write your covering letter. This should be brief – don't go over the page – but you can pick out just one key point to emphasise apart from the general *'Please find enclosed. . .'* stuff. Make sure your enthusiasm for the job comes across. Find something which is linked to the ad itself, and which is clearly important to the employer, for example:

> *You mention that foreign languages are important in this job. This appeals to me particularly as I lived in Germany for two years, and my mother is Spanish, so I enjoy speaking both languages fluently.*

This may also be an opportunity to justify a very under-qualified application. You don't want to draw attention to general shortcomings, but if the employer is bound to notice that far from the degree they asked for you don't even have any A levels, or that you have never worked in the industry, you might as well mention it here and have a chance to justify it:

You'll see that I haven't worked in the catering industry before. However, cooking and entertaining have always been great interests of mine, and for some time I've been looking for the right job to bring my marketing skills to an industry that I really want to be part of.

The interview

The first thing you need to prepare for is that the interviewer is going to ask you about precisely those requirements which were in the job ad. They were there because these points were particularly important to this job, so it would be surprising if the interviewer didn't probe them. This means you have a big clue as to what questions to prepare for.

You need to go into any interview armed with anecdotes: real examples of your past experiences to illustrate the points you want to make. If you want to show that you're honest (if that was a requirement in the ad), practise telling the story of that time you found a wallet left behind after a launch party, and returned it to the customer it belonged to.

Suppose the ad says that you need to be 'able to motivate people'. Remind yourself of the details of that chap on your team a couple of years ago who you inherited and who was notoriously unco-operative, until you recognized that he was a loner and got on really well so long as he was given tasks which he could do alone.

These anecdotes and examples should be the cornerstone of your interview, and the recruitment ad tells you in effect what examples you're going to need. So make sure they're well prepared, and practise them either on your own or role-playing with friends.

A two-way process

Finally, remember that an interview cuts both ways. The employer needs to impress you, otherwise you may turn the job down when they offer it to you. So ask whatever questions you need to.

You'll find as you go through this book that many of the words and phrases listed have a hidden meaning. For example, asking for applicants to have a good sense of humour is generally a sign that the job is highly stressful in some way, and you won't get through the day without being able to laugh.

These hidden meanings are highlighted, together with ways to get to the bottom of the real meaning. So make sure that you take your turn at asking what *you* need to know. After all, with the advice in this book to add to your own natural talents, you could well find yourself having to choose between several job offers. Now that's what I call a successful candidate.

PART ONE

PERSONAL

QUALITIES

'innovative'

aka: creative

This is a job which requires you to be creative. You won't be doing routine work, but dreaming up new ideas and ways to tackle projects from a new angle. In one way, you're onto a winner here because anyone can be creative and innovative, you just have to know how. There are some excellent books on business creativity around, and if this job is important to you, you'd do well to invest in one of them.

Essentially, innovation is all about finding new ways of thinking about problems and challenges. Get hold of a book on the subject, and try a few of the techniques for yourself. Maybe you could experiment on this potential employer's products or customer service, and see if you can dream up some innovative approaches to impress the interviewer with.

There is a slight difference in emphasis between 'creative' and 'innovative', in that innovation tends to imply coming up with new ideas, whereas creativity can mean this, but may also mean creative problem solving (see page 147).

Demonstrating it on paper

Highlight in your application any times you've used your creative skills to propose or introduce new ideas. These may be new products, marketing campaigns, internal systems, customer service improvements. . .don't limit yourself. Any kind of creative thinking will demonstrate that you can be innovative.

Demonstrating it face-to-face

As well as having anecdotes prepared to illustrate all those experiences you've included in your application, you should also be ready to answer questions about innovation generally. These may be wide-ranging, so you need to learn your subject and prepare well. For example, you might be asked:

- 'What techniques would you use to be more innovative in your job?'
- 'How would you define innovation?'
- 'Tell me how you'd go about generating creative new product ideas.'

'ambitious'

aka: keen to progress, keen to develop your career, a zest for achievement

It's not just that they want to promote you – they want to know that you are hard working, bright, and focused on meeting or exceeding your targets. Since all these added together amount to ambition, that's how they sum it up. But their focus is on your dedication to your work more than on your promotion prospects as such.

Hidden meaning

Occasionally, this can signify that the organization you're applying to for a job has a cut-throat culture, in which colleagues compete against each other in a way which can be unpleasantly serious. You could end up having to choose between, for example, losing a promotion or trampling on a colleague. If you don't enjoy this kind of working atmosphere, you need to find out if this is the case.

Key question

Ask the interviewer a question along the lines of: 'How competitive is the company culture between colleagues?'

Demonstrating it on paper

The best way to show you're ambitious and achievement orientated is to indicate that you've been promoted fast in the past. So make sure you clearly show any promotions – list them separately so they are clear. In other words, don't put:

September 2001 – January 2003 ABC Company, Sales Assistant, then Sales Manager. Responsibilities included. . .

Much better to separate out the two so the promotion can't be missed:

March 2002 – January 2003 ABC Company, Sales Manager. Responsibilities included. . .

September 2001 – March 2002 ABC Company, Sales Assistant. Responsibilities included. . .

If you don't have any fast promotions to flag up (or even if you do) you can still demonstrate big successes. So indicate the fact that you've pulled off a major deal, completed a successful project or exceeded targets.

If you're a school or university leaver and have no professional experience, you can still demonstrate ambition in other ways. Maybe you were a prefect or a head boy or girl, or perhaps you captained a school sports team (mention your big successes), or won school or university competitions. Really strong results in academic exams indicate ambition as well as hard work and ability.

Demonstrating it face-to-face

Enthusiasm for your work needs to come across strongly when you talk to the interviewer, so sit slightly forward in your seat and sound genuinely interested in what you do. Have plenty of examples of past successes ready to quote.

If the interviewer asks you why you're leaving your present job, or why you're applying for this one, give answers which indicate that you are ambitious. You might say that while you thoroughly enjoy your present job, it doesn't have the prospects you want to progress your career quickly. This job appeals because it has plenty of challenge and will give you the chance to move up the career ladder as fast as your ability allows.

You can pretty well assume that your interviewer is going to ask you those classic questions along the lines of: 'Where do you see yourself in five years' time?' You want to be careful how you answer this because, if you give a specific goal and the interviewer knows they cannot fulfil it, they will be put off hiring you. So keep it open. But remember that they want to know you have drive and will keep increasing your value to them. Say something like: 'I'm certainly ambitious, and I like to keep moving and progressing. But you can't fit a job to a preset list of conditions. I find it's far more rewarding to let the job lead you forward.'

Another common, and equally tricky, question for the ambitious is: 'When would you expect promotion?' Don't give a firm timescale here. The answer is, you should expect promotion when you deserve it. 'I would hope to be promoted once I have demonstrated my value to the company, and shown that I'm worth it.'

And show how this job suits your long term aims: 'That's why I want to join a company that is growing so that the promotion opportunities will be there when I'm ready to move up,' or 'That's why I want to join a large organization so there are plenty of opportunities when I've gained the skills and experience.'

'determined'

aka: determinaton to succeed

You'll generally find this requirement in ads for sales staff, especially when you'll be cold calling. What it means is that you need to be positive and not to give up in the face of rejection. Many people become quickly demoralized when they are on the receiving end of a series of 'no's. If you're one of them (and there's no shame in it) you probably won't be happy in this job.

Hidden meaning

The fact that you may have to deal with rejection when you're cold calling is hardly a secret. But you may want to consider the extent of the rejections. If you're trying to sell advertising space in an engineering trade publication to engineering firms, you'll probably get a reasonable level of take-up which will keep you motivated. However, selling double-glazing to randomly selected householders will probably get a much lower response rate coupled with a moderately high level of abuse (at least it will if you call me).

▶

> **Key questions**
>
> If you know what you're selling and to whom it will help you assess how successful you're likely to be, so ask for this information if the interviewer doesn't volunteer it. It will also help to know the rate of sales you can expect, so ask: 'What is the average success rate your sales people have at the moment?'

Demonstrating it on paper

The thing which will give the employer the impression you have the determination they're looking for is any sign that you've worked against the odds in the past and stuck at it. Any sales job with a relatively low success rate, such as selling advertising or cold calling generally, will impress them.

On top of that, anything which suggests you have a determined personality will also help. So if you mountaineer or absail in your spare time, or have any hobby which demands determination, say so.

Demonstrating it face-to-face

These kinds of sales jobs have a very high staff turnover, which costs the employer money every time someone leaves. So what your interviewer really wants is reassurance that you will stick at the job. And the best way to reassure them is to show that you understand what it's really like. So be ready to talk about any past experiences of working in demoralizing jobs – preferably similar to this one – and show that you persisted.

You may also be asked about your mental approach to this sort of job, so think about what you can tell the interviewer to persuade them that you have the right attitude. In particular, focus on how the positive feelings when you succeed outweigh the negatives. This will help convince them that you will not only stick at the job but also clinch the sales they need.

'energetic'

aka: stamina

This implies a significant workload which you need to be able to cope with. It may be that you will set your own pace so you need to be able to get through plenty of work each day, or it may be that the job is physically demanding – maybe visiting several sites a week, or doing something exhausting such as running exhibition stands.

Hidden meaning

The potential dark side to this requirement is that this is a company which employs too few staff so that they are constantly overworked. A high but manageable workload can be challenging and even exhilarating, but an impossible workload is simply depressing.

Key question

Try to elicit more information by asking: 'How heavy is the workload?'

Demonstrating it on paper

You want to come across as one of those people who can happily do several things at once – or at least in quick succession. So bring out anything in your CV which shows you have this skill. Maybe you've done this kind of intense job before, or perhaps you simply have more hobbies than most people could fit into their lives. If you really are a high energy person, the chances are you'll have plenty of examples of it to give.

Demonstrating it face-to-face

No one's going to believe you're energetic if you have a limp handshake, never meet their gaze, and speak in a mumble. This doesn't mean you have to bound into the interview room half out of breath, but you do need to exhibit plenty of life and enthusiasm.

Beyond that, have plenty of examples of your ability to cope with a physically or mentally demanding workload. As well as work examples, you can add plenty of others; for example, if you have children you can point out that being a parent with a full time job and a house to run isn't possible unless you have plenty of energy.

'hard working'

aka: diligent

There's plenty of work to get through in this job, and the employer doesn't want you gossiping over the coffee machine or turning up late every morning. This rather serious sounding requirement implies that this is one of those jobs where you'll be expected to get your head down and get on with it.

This says quite a lot about the culture of the organization. Interestingly, statistics show that as many as 70 per cent of people who leave a job within the first year do so because the corporate culture didn't suit them. So you need to assess whether this is the kind of organization you want to work for.

Demonstrating it on paper

A well laid out application which isn't too chatty and informal is probably your best bet here (although take into account the tone of the rest of the recruitment ad). If you're relatively fresh out of education, strong academic results will indicate that you're hard working.

You should also flag up any other experience of the kind of intensive work that this employer seems to have in mind for you. So you might put, for example:

> *February 2001 – March 2003 ABC Company, Sales Executive. Responsibilities included managing my own time to generate month on month growth in sales. . .*

Demonstrating it face-to-face

It's a good idea to dress on the sober rather than the flamboyant side here. The words hard working alone don't necessarily mean this is a puritanical organization, so don't go over the top. Nevertheless, unless the rest of the ad suggests otherwise, this could be a fairly serious kind of culture and you need to look as if you'd fit in.

Obviously you need to have plenty of instances ready to show that you're prepared to work hard. Make sure you come across not only as being a hard worker, but also as someone who actively *enjoys* hard work.

Whatever you do, don't ask any questions at the interview about working hours, or anything else which implies you don't want to work too hard. You can ask all those questions later, after they offer you the job and before you accept it.

'committed'

This word often crops up in ads for jobs such as telesales, and what it almost always means is that the employer wants someone who is going to stay in the job and not leave within a few weeks or months.

Hidden meaning

You have to ask yourself why the employer thinks there's a likelihood that you'll want to leave. Presumably their staff turnover is high. Why? Maybe it's one of those jobs which only a few people are suited for, and maybe you're one of them. If so, great. But if it's not the job for you, you need to know.

The most likely problems, especially in a telesales job or something similar, will be:

- The success rate for sales is low so the job is demoralizing.
- There's very little reward, which is demotivating – maybe there's a modest salary and a promise of commission which is in fact almost impossible to achieve.

> - There's little in the way of support or training from the organ-
>   ization.
>
> **Key question**
>
> You'll need to ask questions to reassure yourself about any of
> these points which concern you. For example:
>
> - 'What is the average hit rate for sales?' If they tell you what the
>   top performers are getting, ask again what the *average* is.
> - 'What is the average commission your sales people earn?'
>   Again, make sure they tell you the average, not the top rate.
> - 'What training will I get?' and 'What promotion opportunities
>   are there?'

Demonstrating it on paper

The most important thing you can do at the application stage
is to show how long you've stayed in past jobs. If you've
changed jobs every few months, you're going to have to come
up with some pretty good reasons for leaving each one. You
can briefly outline *'Reasons for leaving'* at the end of each entry.

If you have spent a good couple of years or more in each job,
make sure your application is set out so that this shows up
clearly, as it's a strong point in your favour with this employer.

Demonstrating it face-to-face

You'll need to show the interviewer that you're the kind of
person who feels that once they're in a job, they're committed to it. You don't take jobs on trial – you don't take them at
all unless you're sure. It would be great if you have an exam-

ple of having had second thoughts about a job in the past after you'd started it, but stayed anyway and found it was the right thing to do. Any anecdotes of this kind which show that once you've said yes, you're committed, will help you.

'drive'

This usually goes together with lots of other words such as 'ambition' (page 5), 'dedication' (page 21) and 'enthusiasm' (page 93). What the employer ultimately wants is for you to drive yourself rather than them having to stand behind you pushing you onwards. So they want you to motivate yourself to meet and exceed your targets without input from them.

This in itself doesn't generally imply that they will be totally uninvolved (although obviously that can happen occasionally). Even very supportive employers may want driven employees. The point is that if you are driven to succeed *and* they are supporting and motivating you, you'll achieve outstanding results between you.

On top of that, there's an implication that you'll be relatively independent so that they will agree targets with you and help you towards them, but you'll motivate yourself day-to-day and generate your own ideas of how to succeed.

Demonstrating it on paper

People who are driven tend to go that extra mile. So as well as the usual guidelines about bringing out relevant experience in your application, it's also worth making a point of doing more than the other applicants have. For example, you might research the organization you're applying to thoroughly and indicate in your covering letter that you've taken this initiative. For example:

> *I see from your annual report that profits have increased by at least 7 per cent year on year since 1998, which makes yours the kind of achievement oriented company I'd like to be part of.*

This indicates that you're interested in success (rather than simply paying the mortgage), but it also shows that you care enough about this job to do your research thoroughly.

Demonstrating it face-to-face

Clearly you need to talk with enthusiasm about your work. Use examples and anecdotes to show that you are target oriented, and let the interviewer see that achievement is vital to your sense of job satisfaction.

This interviewer is likely to ask you questions about your ambitions (see page 5), and also about how self-motivated you are (see page 123).

'dedicated'

This essentially implies a combination of hard work and commitment. This employer wants you to know that the company culture is one where people get their heads down and get on with the job. They also want you to understand that they expect you to care about the job – they don't want any clock-watching or trying to get away with the minimum effort. This is serious stuff.

Demonstrating it on paper

You'll need to show this employer that you take your work seriously. Anything you can highlight to show that you're in the habit of going that extra mile at work will help. For example:

- Working extra hours (without overtime).
- Doing tasks outside your remit.
- Coming up with ideas for improvements (when it's not part of your job to do so).

This kind of thing all goes to show that the job is important to you, and you'll put in whatever effort it takes to get the job done well, rather than putting in only the effort required of you on paper.

Demonstrating it face-to-face

Obviously you should have ready plenty of examples such as those in your application, to reassure the interviewer that if they offer you the job you'll put everything you've got into making a success of it.

It will also help to demonstrate that you're focused on results; the point is not to spend umpteen hours at work, or to get through the day's tasks – the point is to achieve the results that the company needs. This shows that you're in tune with the company's attitude, and you realize that you must be dedicated to the organization, not to the job description.

You can illustrate this in the way you express the examples you pick to show your dedication. For example: 'I had actually assembled all the costs for the project by the end of the day. But I felt that there must be a more cost effective approach, so I puzzled over it on my way home, and when I came into work the next morning I had the solution. . .' See? This shows that you weren't simply doing the job you were asked, but you cared enough to do even better.

'integrity'

This basically means that the employer is looking for someone with sound ethical principles. Now, most employers would prefer their staff to be ethically principled, but this one cares enough to mention it in the recruitment ad. Almost certainly, this is a job which involves working with either the law or people's confidences, or both. Perhaps the employer is a divorce lawyer, and you'd be privy to highly personal information about clients, or maybe the job is as an administrator for a counselling service.

Demonstrating it on paper

You can't really prove integrity without actually putting it to the test. You can prove whether or not you have two A levels, or whether you worked for the ABC Company for six months last year. But no one's going to say: 'Ah, if it's integrity you're after, better not give the job to me.' So this employer can only hope for clues; they won't be expecting firm proof.

In an ideal world, you'll have done a job in the past which has called for this kind of integrity, and you can say so. If this is the case, give your ex-manager from this job as a referee if you can. Or maybe you've done relevant voluntary work – perhaps as a counsellor or a Samaritan. Even if this was with an organization that likes you to keep quiet about it, you can still say you've worked, for example, as a counsellor for a national charity. You can be more open if you're asked in the interview.

If you have no obvious relevant experience, don't worry. As I say, this employer isn't expecting any more than clues at best. If they find nothing to indicate your integrity either way, they'll assess you on other criteria and wait until the interview to form a judgement on this.

Demonstrating it face-to-face

As well as arming yourself with examples and anecdotes which demonstrate your integrity, you should also be prepared to ask questions along the lines of: 'What do you think integrity means?' The interviewer may give you a hypothetical situation which is ethically tricky, and ask what you would do in such circumstances. If you get this kind of question, always err on the side of keeping confidences. If the question allows it, you can always say you'd consult your boss rather than take such a difficult decision on your own.

If you have done work in the past which called for integrity, your interviewer may try to test you by asking you to give away more than you should. For example, suppose you have been a Samaritan volunteer, they may ask you a question about the kind of calls you received. The correct response to this is a friendly: 'I'm afraid I can't talk about that.' This confirms that you can, indeed, keep a confidence.

'entrepreneurial'

Entrepreneurs run their own businesses, and this employer wants someone who can virtually be left alone to run themselves. Generally this will involve projects rather than routine-based work. The employer wants you to:

- Be relatively independent apart from agreeing targets and policies.
- Be able to set your own priorities and organize your own workload.
- Generate your own ideas in order to meet your targets.
- Be able to motivate yourself.

Demonstrating it on paper

This boss wants to see that you can get on with things on your own, without their having to push you and guide you constantly. So anything you have done in the past which shows this will be helpful. If you've run projects, or worked independently of colleagues – from home, in an isolated location or even on the road – this is all worth flagging up.

It's also worth mentioning any activities outside work which show that you can get projects off the ground on your own. Maybe you've started a local group, run a small business on the side, or raised funds to go abroad during your gap year.

Demonstrating it face-to-face

Obviously you need to be ready with plenty of examples of the kind of entrepreneurial experience you've had in the past. It's also worth considering that entrepreneurs are seen as being enthusiastic and energetic people. This may not be a fair perception, but this interviewer is more likely to believe that you are entrepreneurial if you come across as enthusiastic (see page 93) and energetic (see page 12).

'professional'

Whatever job you're applying for you should be professional. So what does this employer really mean? There are all sorts of professional behaviours, from good time-keeping to not gossiping, from efficient message-taking to not fiddling your expenses. Just about every employer would say, if asked, that they require all of these. This employer is concerned with a particular aspect of professionalism, and you'll probably need to pick up clues from the rest of the ad to see what precisely they want.

For example, suppose the ad is for a sales executive, and says: *You will need to be a car owner. This varied role requires someone who is professional, has enthusiasm and can work on their own initiative to tight deadlines.* Presumably you'll be out on your own a lot of the time, and will need to schedule your work yourself, and stick to deadlines without anyone to keep an eye on you. So the kind of professionalism this employer wants is the kind that drives you to meet high standards in time-keeping and meeting targets, even when there's no boss on the spot to check up on you.

It's generally pretty easy to work out what 'professionalism' means when you consider it in the context of the ad as a whole.

Demonstrating it on paper

You really need to do this by demonstrating all the other requirements that surround this one in the job ad. So, in the example above, you'd need to highlight your ability to schedule your own time, work to deadlines and so on.

On top of this, however, you will also need to make sure that your application looks thoroughly professional or you'll undermine your credibility severely:

- Use proper writing paper for your covering letter, or produce it on a word processor printed out on proper clean A4 paper. If you use personal writing paper, have nothing printed on it other than your name and address – no pretty pastel coloured paper with flowers on it or anything else of the sort.

- Your CV should certainly be printed onto clean A4 paper. If you don't have access to a computer, find someone who has or pay a secretarial service to produce your CV and then get it professionally photocopied.

- If you are filling in an application form from the employer, decide what you want to say in each reply before you write it down. If necessary, write it out elsewhere first while you settle on the precise wording. That way, you'll be able to write your final version with no crossings out or corrections. Likewise, make sure you know how to spell each word before you write it down on the application form.

- Check your letter and CV several times for spelling or grammatical mistakes. If you're not that hot on such things, get someone else to check it thoroughly for you.

- Make sure your letter, application and CV are nicely laid out. They should be neat, well balanced on the page, and not all squashed up at the top of the paper.

Demonstrating it face-to-face

Again, you really need to concentrate on demonstrating the requirements that go with the word 'professional'. On top of that, you need to be well turned out, reasonably confident and have facts and answers prepared so that your interviewer is impressed with your professional appearance, behaviour and manner.

You'll find some helpful tips on how to present yourself professionally in Part III: Personal image (see pages 91–116).

'reliable'

Maybe this employer has been let down in the past. Or maybe they're just worried they will be. Whatever the reason, they are concerned to find a candidate who isn't going to let them down in future. This generally refers to two areas in particular:

- They want you to be a reliable time-keeper and to turn up for work unless you really are too ill to get out of bed (and preferably then, too).

- They want to know that once you've been given a task you'll do it without having to be reminded. What's more, you'll do it on time and to at least the standard they expect.

These two are actually related, in that few people are reliable in one sense and not the other. So whichever one really concerns this employer, you need to prove you're reliable in every sense to convince them that you're reliable in the sense they care most about.

Demonstrating it on paper

If you have a particularly good time-keeping record, why not say so? At the end of each job entry, you could add *number of days' absence: two* or whatever. So long as this is accurate and verifiable, it will reassure the employer that you are the reliable type.

You can also flag up any responsibilities which have included strong reliability. For example, if you've worked as an accounts supervisor, you could list under responsibilities: *submitting weekly figures by 5.15pm each Friday without fail*. This emphasizes that you're used to being relied on, and you can live up to it.

Demonstrating it face-to-face

You'll need to show that you understand the impact your performance has on other people – this is the crux of the issue after all. You need to be reliable because other people can't do their jobs unless you do yours. So try to find an instance where you have had to make an effort to meet expectations, but explain that you did so because you realized what the consequences would be for everyone else if you didn't.

You don't want to pick an example where it was your fault that you had to make the effort. On the other hand, you don't want to be seen to blame another individual either – that doesn't make you look good. So find a situation where it was no one's fault, for example:

- You were ill but went in to work for half a day just to get this essential task done.
- Someone let you down through no fault of theirs – they went into labour unexpectedly, or their flight back from a foreign trip was cancelled.

- You were let down by a system rather than a person – there was a postal strike or a computer crash.

'mature'

This is effectively a coded way of saying that this employer doesn't want to employ anyone too young. If you're sixteen, you're unlikely to get any jobs which ask for someone mature, even if you're actually very sensible for your years.

So why does this employer want a 'mature' employee? The general perception is that older staff are more reliable, likely to stay longer in the job, more sensible, less likely to muck around on the job, and less likely to turn up at work with a hangover (if at all). You may or may not agree with this assessment, but the chances are that these are the qualities this employer is after.

The other possibility is that the job involves working with young people and the employer feels that an older person in this post will command more authority. So if the ad is for a university bursar, or a school administrator, it may be that an air of authority which children and young people will respect is what the employer is really after.

Demonstrating it on paper

Your age is going to be the biggest clue for this employer, and there's not a lot you can do about that. In addition, list your hobbies and think about what they say about you. Which of the following lists of hobbies do you think seems the more mature?

- Reading, walking, listening to music.
- Hang-gliding, movies, motorbikes.

Don't lie, but present your hobbies in the way which will appear most mature. 'Listening to music', for example, sounds better than 'Rock and roll' for this job although it might mean exactly the same thing.

Demonstrating it face-to-face

Your appearance and natural personality will say a lot about you. This might not be the time to wear that yellow tie with purple stripes. On the other hand, just because the interviewer wants someone mature, that doesn't mean they're necessarily looking for a serious, sober person. Unless there's some other indication of this (it's a job at a funeral parlour, for example) there's no need to go over the top.

So long as you reach the basic level of maturity the interviewer is looking for, they'll want to focus on your suitability for the job in other ways. So don't get hung up on appearing super-mature; just concentrate on demonstrating that you can actually do the job.

'honest'

You'll probably find this in an ad for a job where there is more scope than usual for dishonesty, for example a financial supervisor. It's generally pretty obvious why the employer is making a point of mentioning it.

Demonstrating it on paper

Employers know perfectly well that honesty is not an easy quality to determine in a job applicant. Your CV is hardly likely to trumpet the fact that you're dishonest – not that *you* are, but some people are and it still doesn't get a mention on their CV. (I suppose they have to lie about it on their CV precisely because they're dishonest.)

Anyway, this employer is never going to expect more than clues to your honesty, so the more clues you can give, the better. The kind of things which suggest honesty to an employer are:

- Previous jobs where honesty was important, especially if you give that employer as a referee.

- Being treasurer (or some similarly trustworthy post) of any organization.

- Any religious activities (this isn't strictly a guarantee, of course, but rightly or wrongly it gives an impression of honesty). So if you're a lay cleric of some kind, or you run a bible study group, make sure you say so.

- Any role where you have a position of authority or respect, such as being a member of your local round table, or a school governor. (Again, we all know this proves nothing, but it still counts in your favour.)

Demonstrating it face-to-face

Certain kinds of body language can suggest a less than honest nature. The trouble is, some of these can be similar to the kind of body language that accompanies shyness or nerves. Since your interviewer is only going to take in such messages subliminally, you need to avoid the following:

- Lack of eye contact.

- Looking at the floor.

- Excessive fidgeting.

- Defensive posture (such as arms and legs folded).

The occasional lapse probably won't matter, but if you demonstrate too many of these signs your interviewer may get a feeling that you're not trustworthy. For this interview, this could cost you the job.

Apart from your body language, you need to think about what examples you can give from your past to demonstrate your

honesty and trustworthiness. As well as preparing these anecdotes, be ready for the interviewer to ask you to tell them
about a time when your honesty has been put to the test.

'dynamic'

This is really about a combination of energy (page 12) and drive (page 19). The implication here is that if you get the job you should hit the ground running. You won't need any help to get excellent results: your natural energy will propel you inexorably towards your targets and beyond.

This requirement generally goes with the kind of job in which you make your own work – run your own projects, maybe, or at least set your own pace.

Demonstrating it on paper

Your past experience will show how dynamic you are, so you need to bring out the most relevant data to emphasize this. You're looking for anything which shows you've either:

- Set your own agenda, or
- Exceeded targets.

Setting your own agenda might mean running projects, being in charge of a self-contained team, or setting up new initiatives – from a company newsletter to a village football team. Dynamic people start out that way, so school or further education experience may be relevant too; if you're a school leaver or a new graduate it certainly will be. If you directed the school play or organized the Scouts' camping trips, it all indicates a dynamic personality.

When it comes to exceeding targets, you want to highlight everything from exceptional academic results to beating your work targets in previous jobs.

Demonstrating it face-to-face

You might be the most dynamic person in the world, but the interviewer's never going to believe it if you slouch into the interview, look at the floor and mumble your answers. You need to show you have energy and enthusiasm if you want to impress this interviewer. Don't try to act something you're not – that never works – but if you're dynamic enough to do this job you're quite capable of showing it. Just remember to:

- Make eye contact.
- Speak clearly.
- Sound confident.

As well as preparing examples of times you've shown drive and energy, you should also be ready to answer a question along the lines of: 'What do you think we mean by dynamic?' There isn't a single correct answer to this question – obviously it's about energy, drive, self-motivation and so on. The point is to answer the question with confidence and to look as though you've thought about it. If you um and er your way through an answer it won't impress the interviewer even if the answer tallies with their own definition.

'discreet'

Can you keep a secret? This employer hopes you can. The job evidently involves knowing secrets about people that you mustn't divulge. Maybe you shouldn't even let the person concerned know what you know. It sounds like a job for an international spy, but in fact it could be anything from a bank manager to a doctor's receptionist.

The employer doesn't want you blabbing about who earns what, or who's suffering from haemorrhoids. They need to be sure that you can keep your mouth shut in the interests of clients or colleagues.

Demonstrating it on paper

You need to show that you've been in positions in the past which called for discretion. So flag up any jobs which required sensitivity, and mention that you needed to be discreet. So under 'responsibilities' you should mention something like *maintaining confidentiality over clients' financial affairs*.

Mention any relevant experience outside work, too, from meals on wheels to being a member of the PTA, explaining why you needed to be discreet.

If you can, give referees who can vouch for your discretion.

Demonstrating it face-to-face

You should be ready with anecdotes of times in the past when you've been under pressure to give away information you didn't feel you should. Needless to say, you should be able to reassure your interviewer that you didn't buckle.

The interviewer may try to test your discretion by asking you a hypothetical question. Suppose you're applying to be a hospital department manager – they might ask something like: 'What would you do if an elderly patient's daughter rang up on her behalf wanting the results of her mother's recent tests?' They're unlikely to warn you this is a question to test your discretion, as the correct answer would then be obvious. So be ready for this kind of question in disguise as a question about something else, such as your knowledge of procedure.

If you're asked a question of this kind, your answer should always tend towards discretion. In the case above, you wouldn't give the results to the daughter unless you'd been authorized to do so. It's a good idea to say that you would ask for guidance from your boss (probably the interviewer themselves), but if they weren't available you would err on the side of discretion until you could seek their advice.

'loyal'

aka: loyal and committed

Personally, I don't actually think this requirement belongs anywhere in a job ad. You don't get 'loyal' people and 'disloyal' people. Everyone is quite capable of being loyal if that loyalty is earned, and they won't be if it isn't. If a company wants loyal staff it's very easy – all they have to do is win your trust and respect.

What this employer actually wants is the appearance of loyalty. They want to know that:

- You are trustworthy.
- You'll stay with the company for some time.
- You'll say good things about the company to outsiders.
- You'll do that bit extra from time to time without any direct reward for it – extra hours, extra responsibilities etc.

Hidden meaning

Employers often ask for a particular quality because they've had a problem in the past when they've felt that quality has been lacking. This can be due to an unsuitable candidate having been given the job last time round, but it can be their own fault. If they've had a number of disloyal staff (as they see it) in the recent past, there's a good chance that's because they do nothing to earn staff loyalty. Sadly, there are still companies around which think that loyalty is something you can buy, and staff owe it to them no matter what. These companies, therefore, make no effort to cultivate loyalty among their workforce, and can be demoralizing to work for.

They may also use 'loyalty' as a kind of emotional blackmail to get you to do more than you're paid for. For example, they may expect you to put in extra hours covering for someone who's on sick leave. They won't reward you for the extra effort, but they'll make it clear that if you're 'loyal' to the company you'll do it.

Key question

'I'm pleased that loyalty is an important issue to you: I'm happiest working for a company I feel very loyal towards. What kind of loyalty schemes or strategies do you operate?' The interviewer should either be able to reel off reassuring examples, or they'll fluff about and confirm your suspicions.

Demonstrating it on paper

Any kind of long service is a good thing, so flag up any jobs which you've held for some time. If you can legitimately get the word loyalty into your description of responsibilities for any post, all the better. For example, *showing loyalty to my immediate manager during times of pressure or crisis.*

There's a limit to how clearly you can indicate loyalty in your application, and the employer knows this. So they're not going to select you for interview on the basis of your apparent loyalty, they'll shortlist you for your other skills and assess your loyalty more thoroughly at interview. Demonstrating loyalty in your application is simply a bonus.

It's also worth selecting referees who you feel confident will give you high marks for loyalty if asked.

Demonstrating it face-to-face

You need to be ready to answer questions such as:

- 'Tell me about a time when your loyalty has been tested.'
- 'How would you define loyalty?'

You also need to show total loyalty to past employers. Even if previous managers or organizations have created problems for you, you mustn't criticize them in any way. If you're 'disloyal', the interviewer will assume that you'd talk the same way about them if they became your boss. They may even tempt you, with a question like:

- 'What is your present boss's greatest weakness?'

'Where do I start?' is not the right response to this question. Don't fall for it, no matter how long a list of complaints you may privately have about your boss. Remember, this interviewer may one day be your boss. So tell them what they would like to hear about themselves.

Say something along the lines of: 'To be honest, I'm lucky to have a very supportive boss who is good at her job and very easy to work with.' Then look as if you're really trying to think of a weakness and add: 'I can't think of anything – if I did it could only be something so picky it wouldn't be worth mentioning.'

Alternatively, come up with a weakness which is really a strength. For example: 'He's probably too soft. But then, he has our loyalty so none of his team takes advantage of it.' Your other option – if your interviewer has a sense of humour – is to side-step the question with an answer such as: 'What's his greatest weakness? Probably chocolate.'

'keen to learn'

aka: a desire to learn

This employer is clearly keen to teach. They want to take on someone who doesn't have the necessary skills, and then train them up. Maybe inexperienced staff are more affordable; maybe they don't expect to find anyone with the skills they need; perhaps the job is one of continuous learning – keeping up with the latest technology, for example.

The chances are that this is a good thing from your point of view. Assuming you want a stimulating job rather than one which simply pays the rent, this employer wants you to develop and broaden your skills.

Demonstrating it on paper

Any indication that you've wanted to learn in the past suggests that you'll want to learn in the future. So highlight any training you've undergone at work, especially if you've put yourself forward for it (and make this clear). Outside work, anything from taking a language course to going on adventure holidays will show that you're looking for stimulation and challenge.

Demonstrating it face-to-face

You need to arrive at the interview armed with plenty of examples of new skills you've acquired, especially those you learnt through your own choice rather than because it was part of the job.

The job itself should give you an idea of whether the skills this employer wants to teach you are physical, technical or intellectual. So tailor your examples to suit. For instance, if you're applying to be a logistics manager it's more use to point out that you put yourself through HGV training than that you've enrolled on a 'teach yourself macramé' course.

'authoritative: 1'

This can actually mean one of two things, and you'll need to use the context of the recruitment ad to tell you which. The possibilities are:

- You should sound like an authority in your field.
- You should have natural authority so that people readily do as you tell them. (see page 50 for this interpretation).

It will usually be obvious which of these is required but occasionally – for a job such as a secondary school teacher – it may not be clear. In this case you should aim to be authoritative in both senses.

This employer wants to be sure that you really know your stuff, and also that it's obvious that you do. It's no good being an expert but being so self-effacing that you come across as being unsure of your facts. This is a job where other people – maybe customers or senior management – will need to believe in your authority on your subject, whether it's engineering, computers or marketing campaigns.

Demonstrating it on paper

At this stage, just concentrate on convincing the employer that you *are* an expert. You can't hope to demonstrate that you come across as an authority, but they won't expect that. They'll save that judgement for the interview.

As well as your relevant jobs in the field, list all the qualifications you can, of course. And list any training you've delivered (you *must* be an expert if you've taught the subject). Equally, reports you've written add to your credibility as an expert, so list these too.

Demonstrating it face-to-face

Assuming you *are* something of an authority on your subject, you should have no trouble answering questions on it. You should prepare any anecdotes which you can use to show your expertise.

The main challenge is likely to be making sure you come across as an authority. The interviewer wants to be sure that other people will believe in you as an expert. This is all a matter of presentation, really. You need to talk about your subject with confidence (see page 98), and state facts clearly rather than presenting them as probabilities. Compare the following two statements about running a direct mail campaign:

- 'You can expect a response rate of at least five per cent.'
- 'Well, I'd have thought you'd get at least a five per cent response, I expect.'

Both are saying the same thing in different words. But the first sounds far more authoritative than the second.

'authoritative: 2'

This can actually mean one of two things, and you'll need to use the context of the recruitment ad to tell you which. The possibilities are:

- You should sound like an authority in your field (see page 48 for this interpretation).
- You should have natural authority so that people readily do as you tell them.

It will usually be obvious which of these is required but occasionally – for a job such as a secondary school teacher – it may not be clear. In this case you should aim to be authoritative in both senses.

You need to be able to give instructions in a way that doesn't entertain a refusal. In fact you should be able to ask (rather than tell) in a manner which implies an unquestionable authority. The more naturally authoritative you are, the less trouble you will have with discipline, mutiny or even just plain resistance.

Being authoritative, however, does not mean being domineering. In fact, the whole point of being authoritative is that you don't need to control through fear or by wielding a large stick. The strength of your personality means you can afford to be friendly and supportive without losing control. If you speak as though whatever you say can't be questioned, people don't question it.

Hidden meaning

You're safe here if the ad clearly wants you to be an expert in your field. However, if it seems to call for you to be able to wield authority, you may need to question why. If you'll be in charge of thirty teenagers, it seems like a perfectly sensible requirement. In fact any job which requires you to keep control of large numbers of people could quite reasonably need candidates to be authoritative.

But suppose the job is for a warehouse supervisor, or a shift manager. In this kind of job you would expect your staff to follow instructions without a special need for an authoritative manner. If this employer particularly needs you to be authoritative, is there a discipline problem in the department that you need to know about?

Key question

You'll need to ask the interviewer questions along the lines of: 'What is morale like in the department at the moment?' or 'How co-operative are the staff generally?'

Demonstrating it on paper

You can certainly show that you have held positions of authority – both at work and in your outside activities. This says nothing about your manner, but at least it shows you have the experience. The employer is expecting to wait until the interview to form an opinion on whether you are a naturally authoritative person.

The only other thing which, on paper, can add to a sense that you have a strong personality is if other managers have chosen to give you positions of authority at a young age. If you've been promoted or appointed to a managerial position much younger than is normal, this suggests that you are ahead of your years in being able to exercise authority over a department.

Demonstrating it face-to-face

This is where your interviewer gets to decide for themselves how authoritative you are. Of course, you don't actually want to demonstrate your skills as such: telling your interviewer what to do, or taking over the interview, may show that you have immense authority but it's not likely to encourage the interviewer to warm to you.

You need to express confidence, above all else (see page 98). If you have an air of believing in yourself, other people – including your interviewer – will believe in you. This is perfectly compatible with being warm and friendly, so don't make the mistake of thinking that you need to appear cold or distant in order to seem authoritative.

'pragmatic'

You need to be able to make practical decisions for this job. Isn't that the case with every job? Well, yes. So what's different about this one? Generally, pragmatic decisions are harder for some reason in this job, which is why the employer feels the need to spell it out.

Sometimes it's so easy to get bogged down in theory or ethics that it's hard to make a decision at all. That doesn't mean you should abandon or ignore these ideals, but that you shouldn't lose sight of the fact that you need to make a workable decision and get on with the job.

For example, suppose you've produced a fixed volume of your product – call it tins of beans. You've packaged up several thousand and you're supposed to sell them at 20p a tin. But the bottom has fallen out of the bean market and no one's prepared to pay above 14p a tin. You could listen to the theory that the bean market always recovers, or hold out for a customer prepared to pay more for your particular brand, or you could be pragmatic and just offload the damn things at 14p a tin.

Hidden meaning

If pragmatism means ignoring theory, selling at cut price or making painful decisions about, say, redundancies rather than burying your head in the sand, it's a valuable quality. But sometimes it can mean riding roughshod over the needs of staff, or breaking commitments to small suppliers – in other words behaving in a way you may feel is unethical.

If you have concerns about this, you need to find out what this employer really means before you find yourself in a job where you can't sleep at night.

Key question

'What sort of issues call for pragmatism in this job?'

Demonstrating it on paper

This is almost impossible, except that you want to come across as someone practical rather than idealistic. Also, pragmatism can often mean getting on with any decision rather than waiting indefinitely to find the 'right' decision. So the more you appear practical and like the kind of person who wants to get on with things, the better. So you're better off listing bungee jumping rather than bonsai growing as a hobby.

You can also highlight your experience in taking decisions under the 'responsibilities' sections of your past jobs. Use phrases such as *taking decisions quickly when necessary*, or *executing decisions even when they were unpopular* where this was the case.

Demonstrating it face-to-face

Being pragmatic has a lot to do with decision making – that's where you get to exercise the pragmatism. So prepare plenty of examples of difficult decisions you've taken where you've opted for the most pragmatic course. You can expect to be asked plenty of questions about decisions you've taken in the past and why you've made those particular choices.

'robust'

aka: resilient

You're likely to get a bit of a battering in this job, and you need to be able to stand up to it. Maybe the job is in the DSS and you're going to be an occasional target for abuse from clients, or perhaps the hours are extremely long and you need to be physically resilient to cope.

Hidden meaning

It's often obvious what this requirement is all about but, if it isn't, you'd better find out just why you need to be robust. Otherwise you could get an unpleasant surprise when you find that your staff are belligerent towards authority, or you're expected to spend several hours a day out of doors regardless of the weather or the time of year.

Key question

Simply ask the interviewer straight: 'You mention in the job ad that you're looking for someone robust. What kind of resilience does the job call for?'

Demonstrating it on paper

You need to work out if you can from the job ad what kind of robustness is needed, and then show you have the necessary experience. If it's physical resilience that's wanted, indicate what physical hobbies and activities you practise, and spell out what other physically demanding jobs you've done.

If the job requires emotional robustness, highlight past jobs where you've worked under similar strain. Or maybe you've done volunteer work for a charity such as Victim Support which has called for emotional resilience.

Demonstrating it face-to-face

You'll need to be ready to talk about specific experiences in the past where you've needed to display the kind of robustness in question. Choose anecdotes which show you in a good light, and which indicate that you're used to working under this kind of strain.

'bright'

Defining the word 'bright' is a controversial exercise. What this employer means is that you're going to need to be able to do the kind of things which 'clever' people find relatively easy:

- Debate and discuss complex issues with other intellectually capable people.
- Learn new mental skills, and grasp ideas, quickly.
- Take new information on board easily.

Academic qualifications can be a useful indicator of a certain level of ability, but of course some extremely bright people haven't two GCSEs to rub together. So if your qualifications are lacking, you simply need to find other ways to show you have these skills.

Demonstrating it on paper

Once you get far enough up the academic ladder, you can produce qualifications which will keep this employer happy. A good degree or a high-level technical qualification should be sufficient to reassure them that you have what they need.

If you lack these qualifications, you'll need to highlight other aspects of your CV. Flag up responsibilities in past jobs such as *generating ideas* or *learning new software first to train up other people*. These kinds of skills show that you are bright and able even if you don't happen to have the exam results to prove it.

If your academic qualifications are truly embarrassing for the job you're applying for, you should give a reason (but don't make it sound like an excuse). For example, if you have half a dozen GCSEs and you know most of the other job applicants will have degrees, you can include in your CV the reason you left school at sixteen:

- 1994: *left school to train in theatre design*

. . . or some other reason which shows you had self-motivation and ability, not that you weren't capable of progressing.

Hobbies and activities can say a lot about you (rightly or wrongly in this case). If you want to appear bright, don't go on about cooking or rally driving. Mention instead that you enjoy playing chess, or that you belong to the local reading group. If you mention reading as a hobby, by the way, specify what genre if it helps your case – you don't want them thinking you enjoy blockbusters when you actually read scientific biographies. And *don't lie* – if biographies of 20th century scientists turn out to be one of your interviewer's favourite categories, you're going to look both stupid and dishonest.

Demonstrating it face-to-face

Quite frankly, your interviewer is largely going to assess your intelligence according to their own impression when they meet you. However, you can help by preparing anecdotes – whatever you're trying to illustrate primarily – which also show off your intellectual abilities.

Be ready to talk about all the issues on your CV which demonstrate your abilities, and be articulate (see page 73) and confident (page 98) in the way you discuss them.

The interviewer may decide to test you with a question designed to find out how bright you are. Here are a couple of classics to be ready for:

- 'What do you think about privatization/global warming/ the Middle East question (or whatever)? Whatever the topic, you need to demonstrate in your answer that you can see both sides of an argument, that you don't view things in an over-simplistic way, that you can discuss a subject fluently and that you are capable of making judgements. So don't rant on about your particular views (if you hold strong views) without acknowledging the other side of the debate. You are particularly likely to be asked these kinds of questions by companies to which they are relevant. Pharmaceutical companies may ask your views on supplying cost-price drugs to the Third World; banks might ask your views on interest rates. So take into account their likely view on the subject.

- One of the ways in which interviewers can test you is by asking you more than one question at a time. For example: 'How would you approach a typical project, what is the biggest project you have you handled in the past, and what were the major difficulties you encountered?' Unskilled interviewers may do this unintentionally, but skilled interviewers are more likely to do it as a test of your intelligence. The more of the questions you answer (and you have to hold each one in your head while you answer the others), the brighter they will assume you are. If you repeat the question back to them as soon as they ask it, this will help you to fix it in your mind.

'passionate about business improvement'

Do you really want to see the company you work for get better and better at what it does? And do you honestly care that your customers should be even more satisfied this year than they were last year? Or do you just want to have a pleasant time from nine to five and bank your pay at the end of the month?

This employer wants you to feel strongly that your satisfaction and enjoyment of the job are intrinsically linked to the company's success. In other words, you are emotionally involved in the organization, and therefore care passionately that it should constantly improve. And be aware that while growth is important – and should follow on from improvement – this company is focused on *improving* above all, not on growth at any cost.

Demonstrating it on paper

You can mention this particular phrase in your covering letter, saying how it attracted you to the job because you are passionate about being involved in an organization which is constantly improving.

Use your CV to show how improving the business as a whole is at the top of your priority list. When you list your responsibilities in past jobs, mention anything you can which shows you were focused on this, such as *looking for ways to increase customer satisfaction levels* or *minimizing costs without compromising the quality of the products.* If you think about it, you can find such ways of accurately describing many tasks – it's simply a matter of looking at it in terms of the improvement of the whole business.

Demonstrating it face-to-face

Think about the word 'passionate' if it appears in the job ad. This employer didn't want you to be 'concerned' or 'interested', but 'passionate'. So you'll need to come across as enthusiastic (see page 93) about finding ways to make businesses grow and improve.

As well as talking about your past experience and interests, with a ready supply of anecdotes to illustrate your passion for business improvement, you can also impress the interviewer by asking the right kind of questions when it's time for you to put your own questions to them. For example:

- 'Where does the company want to be in five years' time?'
- 'What is the company's top priority for improvement right now?'

PART TWO

COMMUNICATION

'communication skills'

aka: ability to communicate well both verbally and in writing, confident communicator

There are plenty of jobs where being able to talk and write confidently and well is important. If an employer actually bothers to mention this in the recruitment ad, the chances are that this job entails specific tasks which are speech or writing based. So you can expect to have to do at least some of the following:

- Give presentations – even if only informal ones to small groups.
- Write reports.
- Deliver training.
- Draft documents for circulation.
- Argue your department's case coherently at meetings.

You get the picture. This isn't a sit-at-your-desk-and-only-speak-to-your-colleagues kind of job. You'll need to be able to structure a written document or a spoken presentation, lay out written work attractively and clearly, and speak with confidence and a clear voice to groups of people.

Unless the ad states otherwise, there's no reason to suppose you have to be an expert at these things. This employer may be happy to develop your skills, and train you up in the finer points of assembling a report or giving a major presentation to a large group. They just want to know that you have a grounding in these skills, and the potential to build on them.

Demonstrating it on paper

Well, obviously you should be able to show your written skills in your application. This doesn't just mean that it should be correctly spelt and grammatically correct (although it patently should be these things too). It also means ensuring your application, CV, covering letter and anything else you submit should be:

- Coherently structured.
- Clearly laid out.
- Attractive to look at.

This in itself will imply that you are also a good verbal communicator; few people communicate brilliantly on paper and atrociously face-to-face, since both require similar skills – a good understanding of structure, clarity and so on. The only thing which stops a good written communicator from being as effective face-to-face is acute shyness. So to put the employer's mind at rest on this score, highlight any experience you've had in addressing groups of people, from running training sessions or giving presentations to speaking at protest rallies.

Despite making your written skills plain in the way you present your application, you should of course still flag up any relevant experience you have too: writing reports, articles for newsletters or magazines, training materials and so on.

Demonstrating it face-to-face

It stands to reason that your interviewer, who will largely have assessed your written skills on the basis of your application, is now going to form an opinion of your verbal skills from the way you perform at interview. So you certainly need to have a clear speaking voice, and come across as confidently as you can.

You will, however, be asked about your experience in both writing and speaking to groups, so make sure you also have anecdotes and examples ready to quote to reassure your interviewer that you really are as good as you seem.

'able to liaise at all levels'

aka: ability to contribute at board level

Most people can liaise perfectly successfully downwards. So long as you don't patronize, talk over people's heads or appear arrogant, it's easier than liaising upwards. So when an employer asks for this skill, they really mean that they want you to be able to deal confidently and effectively with all levels of management above you.

So what does this mean? There are three aspects to being effective when dealing with board level downwards:

- *Be confident.* The most basic consideration is that you mustn't be phased by talking to board members. Many people, especially in large organizations with several layers of management, are a little nervous at talking to top directors (at least until they become used to it) and that's fine, so long as it doesn't throw you, or make you clam up completely when your voice needs to be heard. You need to have the confidence to express your view – diplomatically of course – even if you think it may be unpopular with some senior people.

- *Understand their perspective.* Senior management have to take a broad view of the organization. They can see beyond the specific requirements of individual departments and are concerned with their vision and strategy for the whole organization. In order to communicate with them effectively, you have to be able to see what they see. When you make recommendations to them or discuss problems, you've got to put things into their language and see the big picture yourself.

- *Don't get bogged down in detail.* By the same token, board members have to deal in policy and strategy, not detail. It's enough for them to decide that a particular department will do a particular thing. They don't want to waste their time discussing *how* it will be done – that's the manager's responsibility. It's not only a matter of their time, either. If they spend too long looking at the trees, they will no longer be able to see the whole wood – and that's what they're there to do. So you need to discuss the big stuff with them and keep the detail for later when you're with your colleagues or line manager.

Demonstrating it on paper

This is quite tricky, but the important thing is to show that you can focus on the big picture. So any experience of setting strategy or of being involved in high level decision making is important. Equally, you need to set out prominently any experience of dealing with senior management. So if you've given presentations to the board, or contributed to directors' meetings, say so.

Demonstrating it face-to-face

The most important thing you can do here is to come across as being totally confident talking to your interviewer, who is of course senior to you. And have examples of dealing with top management ready to hand. If you have dealt with very important customers, this will also demonstrate that you're used to communicating with senior people.

You may also be asked questions such as:

- 'How does contributing to a meeting of directors differ from contributing to a meeting lower down the organization?'

- 'If you were at a meeting with senior managers and one or more of them argued strongly with your point of view, what would you do?'

So be prepared to show that you've thought about the different demands of communicating with senior managers and directors, and that you can answer this kind of question.

'articulate'

What's the point of being articulate? Well, it will help you to get your point across clearly and persuasively when you need to. It will also enable you to communicate on an equal basis with other articulate people. So this employer clearly needs you to do one or both of these things.

Being articulate has nothing to do with being able to impress people with long words and complex styles of speech, so there's no need to be intimidated if you don't have a degree in comparative linguistics. You simply need to be able to talk confidently and express yourself well.

The chances are that this job will entail either selling or nego-tiating (whether internally or externally), and that you'll need to be able to argue your position convincingly.

It may be that the customers you'll be dealing with are all very articulate – perhaps highly educated – and you need to be able to communicate with them on an equal footing.

Demonstrating it on paper

This is another of those skills which the application itself should be able to demonstrate. If your application is well put together using correct English and a clear layout, the strong implication will be that you are an articulate person.

You can build on this if you have any past experience which reinforces the impression that you must be articulate. Whether you have handled tricky negotiations at work, or were a member of your school or university debating society, it all goes to convince the employer that you're the person for the job.

Demonstrating it face-to-face

Any relevant experience is going to be worth mentioning, but frankly your performance at interview is going to account for 99.9 per cent of your interviewer's opinion about how articulate you are. So speak confidently and clearly. Prepare answers and anecdotes to any questions you expect to be asked so that you don't um and er but give polished replies.

Having said that, don't get too hung up about how articulate you sound once you're actually in the interview. If you worry about it too much you'll become too self-conscious to be natural. Assuming you *are* articulate, and you've prepared your answers thoroughly, it will show.

'good interpersonal skills'

aka: good people skills

It's pretty easy dealing with people most of the time, quite honestly. You're nice to them, they're nice to you. . .hardly worth making a point about in a job ad. No, the reason this is being highlighted is because you're going to need to deal with people who may be difficult: angry customers, unco-operative staff, suppliers who are feeling exploited.

This kind of stipulation often appears in ads for jobs such as housing officer or assistant funeral director. In these jobs you would expect to encounter people who are emotional and need careful handling.

For a job with this requirement, you need to be good at dealing with people who are angry, upset or frustrated and helping them to feel that you want to help them. You need to be able to calm down angry clients, and reassure those who are worried or upset. This will mean that you need to be:

- A good listener.
- Able to get to the root of a problem.
- Willing to take the necessary action to sort it out.

Hidden meaning

The danger here is that the job entails dealing with some particularly tricky people. If you've applied to work as a traffic warden, say, this is par for the course. But if this is a job which you don't think should attract difficult customers or staff you need to ask yourself why the employer needs to make a big thing about your people skills. The worry is that you're going to encounter problem customers or staff because of bad practice on the part of the organization.

Maybe their customer service is really poor and complaints are rife. Or perhaps staff are demoralized and demotivated and consequently very unco-operative. This may not be the kind of job you're after at all, so best to make sure what the score is.

Key question

Ask your interviewer: 'What kind of tricky people would I have to deal with?' If they're trying to hide the bad news from you, they are likely to give themselves away answering this question, if only by flustering about the answer.

Demonstrating it on paper

All your relevant experience should be clearly indicated in your application: dealing with customer complaints, handling difficult staff situations (threatened work-to-rules and so on), working with emotional clients and anything else you've done which obviously needed strong people skills.

Demonstrating it face-to-face

The way you come across at interview will give your inter-viewer a lot of clues about your general people skills. You need to be warm and friendly, co-operative about everything from where you sit to what information you give them, and avoid being overly pushy. So don't keep interrupting or trying to take over the questioning.

You'll also need to prepare a few anecdotes demonstrating times when you've handled difficult people effectively, both inside and outside the company.

'exceptional presentation skills'

It sounds like you'd better enjoy giving presentations if you want to apply for this job, because you're likely to be doing a lot of it. Although experience will obviously be a big help here, some people are naturally good presenters who need only minimal extra training to give them polish. If you're one of them, you may get away with relatively little experience so long as you have enough to persuade the employer to give you an interview.

Good presentation skills go beyond simply being able to talk well in public. You need to be able to:

- Structure a presentation.
- Write a good script, full of interesting examples and useful analogies.
- Design effective and interesting visual aids, from props to powerpoint (not just putting up words on a screen and then reading them off).
- Put the presentation together to a deadline.

- Deliver the presentation in a clear and engaging way.
- Follow up it when necessary by clinching a sale.

Demonstrating it on paper

Clearly you need to highlight all your experience of presenting. If this isn't as great as you'd hope, add any other relevant experiences such as:

- Other types of performance (school play, debating society, talks to local groups and so on).
- Report writing (reports are just like presentations, only they're written down. If you can structure and write a good report, you can structure and write a good presentation).
- Organizing events to a deadline.

Just because you've given plenty of presentations in the past, it doesn't mean you're necessarily any good at it. So you also need to quote any successes – presentations which won praise or awards, or which resulted in sales.

Demonstrating it face-to-face

Needless to say, you need to come across as fairly confident (see page 98), and to speak clearly and interestingly. In other words, you need to be plausible as a good presenter, and treat the interview almost as an informal mini-presentation.

You need to talk about your experiences of presentations, and remember that it's not only the way you talk to large groups that counts – it's also the structure and wording of the presentation, and the skilful use of visual aids. So have lots of examples ready to show your interviewer that you appreciate the full range of skills which goes into creating a truly excellent presentation.

It's possible your interviewer may try to get you to give them a kind of mini-presentation as a test. Anything significant you will have been asked to prepare in advance, but they may ask one of those notorious interview questions such as: 'Sell me this pen' (holding up the pen that happens to be lying on their desk).

The key thing here is not to be flustered, but to give the impression that you totally take this kind of thing in your stride.

Give the interviewer four or five benefits of the pen (or notepad, or paperclip or whatever they've asked you to sell them), and then finish, half jokingly, with a standard closing technique: 'Shall I put you down for two dozen?' or 'Would you prefer it in black or red?'

'willingness to deploy tact and diplomacy'

This requires good interpersonal skills (see page 75) but it's more specific. You might well see this requirement stipulated on an ad for a staff liaison manager, or a DSS advisor. The implication is that you're going to encounter a degree of anger or aggression and you need to be able to defuse it. This kind of job isn't for everyone and, if you don't relish the prospect of dealing with these situations regularly, you might be better off giving this job a miss.

The key to being diplomatic in these situations is to show the other person that you are taking them seriously. To do this you need to:

- Hear them out.
- Don't show any aggression towards them or they are likely to respond in kind.

Hidden meaning

This is a perfectly reasonable thing to ask for in an ad for a job which you would expect to demand tact, such as waiting times manager at a busy hospital, or complaints executive at a call centre. You need to worry if you see this in an ad for a job which you don't feel should require any exceptional level of diplomacy. It could mean that the employer knows that their customers or employees are particularly difficult to handle.

Key question

'Why does this job particularly call for a high level of tact and diplomacy?'

Demonstrating it on paper

Demonstrate this by flagging up examples of times you've needed to be tactful and diplomatic. Obviously work experience will be invaluable here, but other experiences count too. Perhaps you run a local organization where you're responsible for turning people down for prestige roles, whether it's running an important event or taking a lead role in the amateur panto. Any demonstration that you can handle sensitive situations effectively needs to be highlighted.

Demonstrating it face-to-face

Clearly the interviewer is going to be interested to see whether you come across as an aggressive or conciliatory type of person. So in general you need to make a point of being co-operative and friendly. You also need to be ready with examples of times you've defused potentially troublesome situations.

If diplomacy skills are high on your interviewer's shopping list, you should expect them to ask you questions on the subject. As well as asking for examples of your own experience, they may well explore wider issues to see how much thought you've given to the matter generally. So be prepared to answer questions such as:

- 'How do you react when you're first approached by someone who looks very angry?'
- 'What skills do you think are especially important for handling people tactfully?'

It's possible that your interviewer might decide to put you to the test by becoming aggressive in their line of questioning and seeing how diplomatically you react. If you become defensive – or buckle under pressure – they won't be impressed. They'll want to see you remain friendly and co-operative but stick firmly to your position.

'good negotiating skills'

The key to good negotiating is to come away with a deal which satisfies your requirements, but which also satisfies the other person. It's called win/win negotiating, and it's the only form of negotiating that keeps everyone happy. If the other person feels you've got the better of them they'll be resentful and demotivated, and their contribution to the deal will be unenthusiastic and grudging.

This employer wants to know that you can negotiate – whether with colleagues, staff, suppliers or customers – in a way which gives *you* a good deal and keeps *them* enthusiastic and committed.

This actually has more to do with psychology than it has to do with the technicalities of the deal. Good negotiators are good communicators who can motivate people and leave them feeling successful. Whether you're a manager getting your team to agree to a minimal salary rise, or a buyer squeezing a good deal out of a supplier, it's creating the feelgood factor which will make you stand out as a negotiator.

Hidden meaning

Generally speaking, this is an honest requirement, especially if you can see that the job calls for plenty of negotiating. But if you can't really see where the negotiating needs to come into play, you'll need to check it out. You don't want to find unexpectedly that, once in the job, your boss expects you to cut your entire team's salaries, or persuade the staff to relocate from central London to Essex.

Key question

Ask the interviewer openly why they are looking for someone with good negotiating skills for this particular job.

Demonstrating it on paper

As usual, highlight in the application any times you've had to negotiate effectively, whether over money or something else such as working conditions or other terms. However, it would be best to avoid drawing attention to times when you have successfully negotiated a better deal out of your boss than they had intended. You don't want this interviewer, as your potential future boss, to feel threatened by your negotiating skills.

Demonstrating it face-to-face

As well as having plenty of relevant instances to hand when your interviewer asks, you should also be ready to answer broader questions about negotiating, such as:

- 'What do you think is the key to a successful negotiation?'
- 'What preparation do you do before you start to negotiate?'

If the interviewer decides to test you by trying to negotiate with you over the salary or conditions for the job (which they might if negotiating is key to the role) you can simply say with a smile: 'I couldn't possibly negotiate the terms unless the job offer was on the table.' This not only pressures them to offer you the job, but also amply demonstrates your skills, since it is a sensible negotiating position to adopt.

'well connected'

What are your networking skills like? This interviewer isn't asking if you're a member of the upper classes; they want to know how many useful people you know. This is partly, of course, because your contacts will be useful for this job. And also because if you already have good contacts you're the kind of person who will make more. And in many professions, good contacts are essential to good business, buying credibility and happy customers.

Hidden meaning

It's not unreasonable to want to employ someone with good networking skills, or even someone who already has good contacts. But asking for someone 'well connected' could mean they want you to bring your contacts with you – in other words to take your customers away from your existing employer.

In some lines of business this is standard practice. Many solicitors, literary agents or hairdressers expect their clients to be loyal ▶

> to them and follow them from employer to employer. But if this isn't that kind of industry, you might feel compromised if this employer wants you to 'steal' clients from your existing employer, and is virtually making it a condition of getting the job.
>
> **Key question**
>
> It should become apparent during the interview if this employer is trying to do anything underhand. But if it doesn't, you can ask: 'You're looking for someone well connected. What sort of connections are you interested in?'

Demonstrating it on paper

Here's your chance to name-drop. You can add a list at the end of your CV headed *Clients include. . .* or *Companies worked with include. . ..* You can also impress by including under 'responsibilities' something like *working with clients at board level* to show that you know the top people, not the minions.

Any networking activities should be included. If you attend lots of business parties and events, say so in your CV. It's one of your responsibilities: *attending business events and liaising with key industry contacts*, for example. You can also list golf under your hobbies, if it is one. It all adds to the image of someone who mixes with the most influential industry people.

Demonstrating it face-to-face

This interviewer will want to know who you know, how well you know them, and in what context you meet them – over lunch, at meetings, to play golf or whatever. They'll also want to hear about your networking: what sort of events do you attend – formal or social? Daytime or evening?

You really need to sprinkle your entire interview with references to your contacts (without making it sound manufactured). So illustrate other skills and qualities with examples which show off your connections. For example, you might be explaining how you saved some huge presentation disaster. The example you choose to give would be the one where you get to say: 'Luckily I knew the MD – he's a member of the same gym as me – so I put in a call and he got back to me within the hour. I asked him if he could possibly change the venue to their larger conference room. . .' Not only have you described how you averted disaster, but you've also added to your networking credentials.

PART THREE

PERSONAL
IMAGE

'enthusiastic'

We tend to think of enthusiastic people as being big and effusive. If this isn't you, don't worry. We all have different ways of showing enthusiasm, and this employer probably isn't bothered how your enthusiasm manifests itself, so long as it comes across clearly.

If you're interested in what you're talking about, and positive about it, you'll appear enthusiastic even if you're the type to be quietly enthusiastic. Why does this employer particularly want enthusiasm in their job applicants, after all? Presumably because they want you to demonstrate the kind of positive feelings which are infectious. Perhaps you'll need to galvanize doubtful customers into believing in the product, or convince demotivated staff that you really are rooting for them. Or maybe you'll simply need to have the enthusiasm to do the boring parts of the job with good grace. Whatever the reason, it is positive interest they're after, so that's what you need to demonstrate.

Demonstrating it on paper

The best way to show your enthusiasm on paper is in your covering letter. If gushing prose isn't you, there's no need to use it. But give some indication of feelings, rather than merely facts. Enthusiasm is largely about putting your heart into what you're doing. Here are two extracts from covering letters – which do you think sounds more enthusiastic?

- 'I enclose herewith my completed application form, and look forward to hearing from you in due course.'

- 'My application form is enclosed; I do hope you'll find it fits the bill. I'd relish the challenge of a job like this and look forward to the opportunity of an interview to prove that I could meet that challenge.'

Both of these are perfectly acceptable sentences to write in your covering letter, but the second will be far more appealing to a manager who is looking specifically for enthusiasm in their applicants.

Demonstrating it face-to-face

Enthusiasm shows in the way you behave in the interview more than anything else. Sure, it's worth preparing examples of times you've carried out boring tasks with a positive approach, or motivated others by the sheer force of your infectious enthusiasm. But actually, your interviewer will decide whether you have the requisite enthusiasm on the basis of how you come across when they meet you. So here are the key tips:

- Sit slightly forward in your seat so that you appear interested – don't slump back if you're in an easy chair.

■ Give full answers to questions to show your interest in them, as monosyllabic answers are never a good idea in interview; if you want to appear enthusiastic they're fatal.

■ Adopt a positive approach even when discussing negative events. This doesn't mean pretending that, for example, you were thrilled to be made redundant from your last job. However, you can still put a positive spin on it: 'I was obviously shocked and worried when I first heard, but actually it turned out to be the stimulus I needed to make a career change and it's worked out really well.'

'friendly'

Well, obviously you're supposed to be friendly. No one's going to advertise for an unfriendly employee, are they? So why is this employer making a point of it? This is going to be a job in which you have to deal with people, almost certainly customers or members of the public, and you'll represent the organization. If you're unco-operative, the person you're dealing with will see the whole organization as unco-operative, just because of you. So you'll need to be friendly in order to give the organization as a whole a friendly image.

Demonstrating it on paper

This isn't an easy thing to show in your application, but there are two things you can do which will help:

- Flag up any experience you have that shows you enjoy meeting and working with people, from running exhibition stands to volunteering in the local soup kitchen.
- Keep the tone of your covering letter relatively informal

(without being over familiar). It comes across as far friendlier to say, for example: 'I was really pleased to learn that you're looking for a customer service advisor, since this is exactly the kind of job I enjoy,' than 'Please find enclosed my application for the post of customer service advisor, for which I would like to be considered.'

Demonstrating it face-to-face

This should be a doddle. If you greet the interviewer with a warm smile and a positive attitude, you'll convince them you're friendly easily enough. Their only reservation may be a concern about whether you can remain that friendly in adversity, so have a couple of anecdotes ready to show that you are as warm and encouraging even when the person you're dealing with is being negative or deliberately unhelpful in response.

'confident'

This is all about being comfortable around people and giving the impression that you know what you're doing. Many shy or underconfident people are very capable, of course, but this employer needs you to *look* capable as well as *being* capable. Perhaps you will meet lots of people and need to chat easily with them, or maybe you'll be giving out information and need people to feel confident in you – which requires you to appear confident in yourself.

Demonstrating it on paper

This is virtually impossible. The only scope you have to sound confident at this stage is in your covering letter where you should use phrases such as *I believe I can do this job well* in preference to something like *I hope you'll give me a chance; I think this job would suit me once I've had the right training*.

Remember that the employer doesn't expect to assess your confidence before interview. You'll be shortlisted on other criteria, and you'll get the chance to show how confident you are later.

Demonstrating it face-to-face

Eye contact is essential here. You need to open with a bright: 'Hello, nice to meet you' (or whatever phrase you feel comfortable with), a warm smile, and a firm handshake. If you're at all nervous about the handshake dance (should I. . .shouldn't I. . .oh, she's going to. . .no she isn't. . .) the solution is simple. You simply decide you're going to shake their hand and you extend yours firmly and confidently. In other words, you take the lead with confidence. Almost certainly, you'll meet their hand already extending but, if they were unsure, you've made the decision for them and they'll respond in kind.

Once you're off to a confident start, keep the eye contact going and don't mumble – speak clearly and know what you want to say (good preparation makes this easy). Avoid underconfident phrases such as 'I think I'm good at this. . .' or 'I feel I can do that. . .'. If you feel too cocky simply saying 'I'm good at this' you can always prefix your remarks with a more confident sounding phrase, such as:

- 'I believe I'm a good manager. . .'
- 'I would say my strongest points are. . .'
- 'My colleagues tell me my greatest achievement has been. . .'

'sense of humour'

probably put 'sense of humour' in the ad because they're fed up with having to replace stressed and exhausted staff on a weekly basis, they should be happy to answer the question. They'd rather put you off now than wait until you've taken the job.

Demonstrating it on paper

On no account attempt to demonstrate a sense of humour on paper. It's completely unnecessary, and will almost certainly backfire. The employer doesn't expect you to demonstrate it at this stage and, in any case, they don't really care about your sense of humour anyway. They were just saying that. What they really care about is your ability to cope with stress, so demonstrate that instead.

Highlight any experience that shows you can work in highly pressured circumstances relevant to the kind of pressure this job seems to involve. For example, if the ad is for a care assistants' leader, indicate times you've worked in demoralizing situations or with people who were in a negative emotional state. If, on the other hand, the ad is for a job as a City trader, you'll need to show you can cope with huge workloads combined with tight deadlines.

Demonstrating it face-to-face

Again, it's not going to be smart to walk into the interview asking: 'Did you hear the one about this guy who goes into a pub. . .?' Remember, the sense of humour stuff is really only a means to an end. What you actually need to demonstrate is how you can work under pressure, with plenty of examples to support what you say.

You may find it helpful to look at the sections, able to work well under pressure (page 144), able to multi-task (page 162), able to prioritize workload (page 227) and, can work to tight deadlines (page 230).

'warm, positive approach'

If you're applying for a job such as, say, a community support worker you may well see this requirement stated in the ad. This is most probably a job in which people may need emotional as well as practical support from you. The employer is looking for someone who enjoys the challenge of helping people feel happier about the problem they have come with. It is most common in ads for jobs which involve dealing with the public, particularly in circumstances where they are concerned about key issues such as employment, housing or children.

Hidden meaning

The downside of the kind of job which calls for a warm, positive approach is that you're likely to find yourself in some emotionally draining situations. You may find this a welcome challenge – many people do – but if it's not your cup of tea you need to find out at this stage how big a part of the job it is.

> **Key question**
>
> Ask the interviewer something like: 'To what extent does the job involve dealing with people who are upset or angry?'

Demonstrating it on paper

You can show you have a warm, caring approach by demonstrating that you have plenty of experience in the kind of jobs which call for this. No one is going to spend a lot of time in these jobs unless they are cut out for it. So highlight any community work, stints at the Citizens Advice Bureau, jobs at hostels for the homeless or anything else that shows you're a warm and caring person.

Demonstrating it face-to-face

You can expect to be asked plenty of questions about your experience working with people who needed a warm, positive approach. You'll probably also be asked about your attitude to people in general, and in particular to the kind of people who this employer deals with. Remember that the ad says not only warm but also positive, so the idea is to leave people feeling that things aren't as bad as they seemed before they talked to you. This positive sense needs to come out in your answers.

Obviously you also need to project warmth in your meeting with the interviewer, so greet them with a warm smile, and show you're a good listener and interested in them.

'outgoing personality'

aka: bright

What this usually means is that you need to be able to talk easily to people you haven't met before. Maybe you'll have to meet and greet clients at events, or perhaps you'll need to cold-call potential customers. Whatever the precise requirements, if you're painfully shy this probably isn't the job for you.

You need to feel comfortable about going up to someone and introducing yourself, and finding something to talk to them about. It's worth saying that many people who are excellent at this will tell you that they were very nervous or uncomfortable when they first started doing it, so it's a skill you can learn. So long as you feel you have the potential to become adept at it, that should be sufficient at this stage.

Demonstrating it on paper

It's tricky trying to get your personality across any more than two-dimensionally in your application. So concentrate on what the employer is really driving at. What they really want is someone who is comfortable talking to and meeting new people – so try to demonstrate this in your application.

Flag up any jobs you've done which involve mixing with lots of people, and meeting people at events, parties or exhibitions. And don't forget out-of-work activities; if you belong to lots of groups that's a pretty sure sign that you're a gregarious person.

Demonstrating it face-to-face

First impressions are important, and your first meeting with the interviewer will count for a lot. The important thing is to be able to chat comfortably with them, especially if you find yourself making small talk before the interview proper starts. If the employer wants to judge how outgoing you are, they may well deliberately engage you in a brief chat before they get into the more serious questions. Here are two tips for making small talk successfully:

- Prepare questions you can ask your interviewer, and subjects you can talk about. These might be to do with the organization, or perhaps the location of the offices or something else relevant. You may find other things to talk about when you arrive – the view, or the building works right outside reception. Pick any topic you like, and let the conversation flow. If it dries up, move on to another topic.

- Remember that people like being asked questions about themselves. Obviously you shouldn't get personal with your interviewer, but you can ask for their thoughts or opinions: 'How do you manage to work with the noise of the roadworks outside?' or 'You must have a beautiful drive into work here.'

You should expect to be asked questions about whether you enjoy meeting new people, and the interviewer is likely to want to know about your experience in this area so have your examples prepared.

'presentable'

aka: smart appearance, well groomed

You should always try to look presentable for any job: it's just a matter of establishing what constitutes 'presentable' for the job in question. Some companies like their staff to look very informal to put customers at ease, while others go for a more traditional smart look.

This is presumably a job which entails meeting customers face-to-face. If you possibly can, go along and take a look at how this company's staff dress. This should be quite easy with a retailer, or even an organization such as an estate agency. You can simply walk into a shop, or stand outside an office at 9am and watch everyone going in.

However, you don't need to be underhand about it. It's perfectly acceptable, if you are offered an interview, to phone up the interviewer's secretary and say that you'd like to know what their dress code is before you come for your interview. They'll be impressed you've made the effort to find out.

Demonstrating it on paper

You don't really need to demonstrate this at all until you arrive at interview. Your interviewer won't be expecting to see any evidence until then. However, if you can show that you've done the kind of jobs which require a smart appearance that will reassure them that you're presentable.

Demonstrating it face-to-face

You need to make an effort for the interview. The very fact that the recruitment ad specified a smart appearance means that you really will be expected to have taken this on board. Here are the key points to make sure you live up to the standard the interviewer is expecting:

- As a general rule of thumb, dress slightly better than the standard dress code for the job. You don't want to be over-dressed, but you want to have made an effort compared with the average employee.

- Make sure you have clean hair, nails and so on.

- Take a comb with you. Ask to use the washroom when you arrive, and check in the mirror that everything is neat and tidy: hair, earrings, tie, buttons, tights, teeth etc. You could also take a spare tie or pair of tights with you in case of accidents on the way to the interview.

'approachable'

This is quite a hard word to define, but basically it's all about being the kind of person people feel easy about talking to or asking for help or advice. It's a criterion often asked for in jobs which involve dealing with the public, who resist talking to people who seem aloof or unsympathetic.

The way to come across as approachable is to be warm, friendly, full of smiles and dressed in a way which people are comfortable with. Check out the dress code for the organization (see 'presentable' page 108) and make sure you're fairly smart; however, don't overdress or people will find you more daunting to talk to.

Demonstrating it on paper

This is one of those aspects of your personal image which is virtually impossible to demonstrate other than face-to-face. However, you can flag up any experience you have in relevant jobs which require a similar image (you'll no doubt be highlighting these anyway for other reasons).

Demonstrating it face-to-face

Obviously you need to come across as approachable from your interviewer's point of view. So be warm and friendly, with plenty of smiles, and be willing to make easy conversation.

If this is an important part of the job (and presumably that's why it warranted a mention in the job ad) your interviewer may also ask you a question designed to elicit your views on it. You may be asked something like: 'What is it that you think makes a person approachable?' You need to have thought about this so you can come up with a good answer, and try to prepare an example from your own experience too, which puts you in a good light. So you can give the general answer, and then say: 'For example. . .' and go into your personal anecdote.

'credible'

If someone wealthy and self-important hires a lawyer to handle a complex libel action for them and a fresh-faced young graduate, still green about the gills, turns up dressed in jeans. . .the client simply won't believe in their ability to do the job. If a potential customer tries to buy a private jet from a sales person who looks as if they'd be more at home selling used cars. . .they'll probably find another supplier. If your washing machine sales person tells you they're an expert in machine technology and then can't work out which is the 'on' button. . .you start to lose faith in them. It's all about credibility.

This employer wants to be certain that you will come across as being plausible in the job they're advertising. They need to feel that their customers will believe in you.

> ## Hidden meaning
>
> This can be a polite or coded way of saying that this employer doesn't want you to be too young, to have too strong a regional accent, to be a woman. Some of these things are more legitimate than others: generally if there is prejudice involved it's a reflection of the customer's prejudice rather than the employer's. But of course occasionally the employer's prejudice creeps in.
>
> There's really nothing you can do about this if prejudice is at the root of it. You may not even get as far as interview – your sex or date of birth may rule you out – or you may lose the job ostensibly on other grounds. Take legal advice if you wish, but legal action is likely to be long and stressful, and won't necessarily succeed. It might be better to console yourself with the thought that you're better off not working for such an employer.

Demonstrating it on paper

The chances are that unless something unavoidable such as your date of birth prevents you getting an interview, the application isn't going to have a strong influence on the employer's perception of your credibility. It's more to do with the way you come across, and they won't know that until they meet you.

Demonstrating it face-to-face

Think about what your employer is expecting the suitable candidate to look like and how they want them to come across. Make sure you dress suitably – don't wear a three-piece suit if you're going to be dealing with teenage customers, or a very short mini-skirt for a job as a school administrator.

You also need to think about your manner. If you're a little younger than is traditional for the job, you need to appear confident to carry it off. Otherwise you'll just look inexperienced. If you're a woman in a man's world, or a man applying for a traditionally female post, you need to adapt your manner so you seem at home in the job regardless.

And when it comes to what you actually say, you need to fight against any signals you may give off unavoidably. For example, if you know people might think you're too young for the job, make sure you counteract this by knowing your stuff backwards.

'exceptional person'

aka: 'special' kind of person, great personality

This is a really tough requirement, because frankly you either are or you aren't what they consider a 'special' person – which might not be what anyone else considers special. I'm almost inclined to advise you to ignore this entirely, since there's nothing you can do about it. They are probably looking for a big personality of some kind, but it's anybody's guess what kind.

Even if you don't feel you have a big personality (whatever that is) it's still worth applying for this job if it looks right for you. For one thing, you may turn out to have just the personality they were looking for after all. And for another, they may decide you have all the more concrete requirements and offer you the job anyway. Even if they don't, the interview practice is still worthwhile. So don't be put off by this.

If the job involves dealing with people who may be in an emotional state (such as a benefits officer, for example) the employer is probably also looking for someone who can be very sympathetic and encourage people to talk about their problems.

Demonstrating it on paper

The only way you can do this is by making your application or your covering letter original in some way. It might be your choice of phrasing (lean towards the informal) or maybe you've got a fancy letterhead, or a red border around your CV. But unless this is your natural style anyway, *don't* take it too far. It's more likely to backfire than anything else.

Bear in mind that although a positive approach like this may help your application, the employer isn't expecting to make a judgement on your personality until they meet you. So your application is not going to be thrown out for indicating insufficient personality. They'll be sifting through and shortlisting candidates for interview on other criteria. Wait until the interview to impress them with your 'special' qualities.

Demonstrating it face-to-face

There's no point pretending to be something you're not. You'll never keep it up (certainly not if you get the job) and it might not be what they want anyway. So be yourself. Within your own personal limits, however, aim to be:

- Warm.
- Friendly.
- Easy to make conversation with.
- And show a sense of humour if you get the chance (and if your interviewer appears to have one).

PART FOUR

iv

WORK STYLE

'flexibility'

aka: adaptability

Some people are sticklers for their job descriptions. 'There's nothing in my job description that says I have to do that. . .'. This employer wants nothing to do with such people. They want staff who are willing to do a few extra hours here, or take on an extra responsibility there.

Sometimes, the ad will be specific about the kind of flexibility that's needed: *may entail some unsocial hours* for example. But often, the implication is that you need an overall flexible attitude. This can be a good thing for a lot of people, because it often implies working as part of a team with a fair amount of give and take – you help them out this week, they'll help you out next week.

Hidden meaning

Many jobs genuinely call for a flexible attitude to fit in with the company culture of all mucking in together when necessary. However, the word is occasionally hijacked by people who ▶

---

actually want to load masses of extra work on you without paying you for it, and then expect you to do it because you knew the job was 'flexible' when you took it.

If your antennae are on the alert for this, the chances are that the interview will either put your mind at rest or deepen your suspicions. If you still have concerns about this by the end of the interview, you need to inquire further.

Key question

Try asking: 'You mention flexibility in your advertisement. Can you tell me what kind of flexibility you're looking for?' This is a perfectly innocuous and fair question, and it should help you to determine whether this employer wants to exploit you or not.

Demonstrating it on paper

You'll need to highlight any flexible jobs you've held in the past, and make this clear under 'responsibilities'. For example, responsibilities should include *standing in for other staff as needed* or *working additional hours when necessary*. If you worked as part of a flexible team, say so.

Demonstrating it face-to-face

Have plenty of examples prepared to show how adaptable and flexible you can be. It helps to mention (if it's going to apply in this job) that you enjoy being part of a strong team and that you feel that can only work if you're prepared to be flexible.

'self motivated'

aka: highly motivated, pro-active, self-starter

The implication here is that you should be able to generate your own enthusiasm for the job. It may be that you'll get plenty of back-up, but this employer is looking for enthusiasm (see page 93) and drive (see page 19) on top of this.

Generally the reason for this is that you won't have a manager around most of the time, so you'll need to keep your enthusiasm for the job going by yourself. Maybe the job involves working from home, or perhaps being out on the road, or simply in an office isolated from your team. You're going to have to generate your own workload, organize it and carry it out. You need to be able to get on and do this without back-up close at hand or day-to-day supervision.

> **Hidden meaning**
>
> The phrase 'highly motivated' is often totally innocent and genuine. Just occasionally, however, it can be a sign that this employer is going to make no effort whatever to motivate you, and ▶

expects you to do it for yourself. Of course, however motivated you are, it's demoralizing working for a company that isn't also motivating you itself. If the interview doesn't reassure you on this point, dig deeper until you're happy that this employer is going to take an interest in you once you're in the job.

Key question

You can start by asking: 'You're looking for someone highly motivated. How involved would you yourself be as a manager?' Their answer may lead you to pursue this line of questioning, but in any case the answer to this alone should give you a good idea.

Demonstrating it on paper

Any time you've worked in relative isolation and still managed to meet or exceed the standard for the job will show that you can motivate yourself. Equally, other activities such as learning a new skill at evening class will show that you can keep going until you succeed even without anyone to drive you.

If this job is going to involve working alone at least some of the time, you should also highlight past experiences of working alone. Mention any hobbies which you do alone, from building model trains to keeping an allotment.

Demonstrating it face-to-face

People who are highly motivated generally display a certain amount of energy. Sometimes the energy is hidden below the surface, but you're going to have to display it in the interview so the interviewer knows it's there. It's not fair, but it's a fact that if you come across as a low energy kind of person, your interviewer will find it a lot harder to believe that you're self motivated. So start with a firm handshake, be bright and confident, speak clearly and make eye contact.

You can assume that this interviewer is going to ask you questions about:

■ Times you've had to motivate yourself.

■ Your techniques for motivating yourself.

■ How you feel about having to motivate yourself.

So make sure you have answers ready for these questions to reassure them that you're highly motivated.

'good team player'

It's clear that this job entails being part of a team, and the employer wants to be sure that you will work well with the rest of the team. Broadly speaking, good teamwork includes:

- Putting the team's needs on a par with – and sometimes ahead of – your own.
- Being flexible.
- Supporting others.
- Being open and communicative.
- Caring about the performance of the team as a whole, and not just yourself.

You don't have to be the world's most gregarious person to be a good team player. Many teams include people who are quiet, or who prefer working alone doing the more self-contained tasks. You simply need to enjoy functioning as part of a group.

Demonstrating it on paper

If you actually are a good team player, your CV should show it (and if you're not, do you really even want this job?). Make it clear on your application or CV which of your previous jobs have involved working as part of a team.

If you're really a natural team player, the chances are you'll have plenty of other experience to highlight too. Whether you play in the local cricket team, help organize charity coffee mornings or belong to the rambling club, it all goes to show that you fit well into a team.

Demonstrating it face-to-face

You need plenty of anecdotes here to show what a good team player you are. You'll be preparing examples of other skills, too, and try to find a few of those which simultaneously show off your teamwork talents. If the interviewer cares enough about your ability as a team player to mention it in the recruitment ad, you can expect to be asked questions such as:

- 'How do you work in a team?'
- 'What do you think makes a good team player?'

'ability to use initiative'

Can you think for yourself? This job calls for someone who can make decisions for themselves without constant reference to their boss. Some tasks are full of decisions, whether small ones or major ones, especially if you work without your manager present most of the time – an office administrator, for example, or a school maintenance supervisor.

In order to use your initiative well, you need to have clear parameters to work within. These will give you the confidence to know what decisions you can make and what options are viable. You also need the support of your boss. No one is going to act on their initiative if they get a rollicking every time they get it wrong. So this employer is going to have to play ball if they want you to live up to their expectations.

Demonstrating it on paper

You should highlight areas of responsibility where you've had to make day-to-day decisions and use your initiative. If you don't state it (under 'responsibilities') it's unlikely to be clear to the employer.

Demonstrating it face-to-face

Your interviewer is more likely to see you as someone with initiative if you appear confident (see page 98). If you wouldn't say boo to a goose, you're not likely to have the courage to take decisions independently.

The interviewer will ask you questions to establish how willingly you use your initiative. So have your anecdotes ready, and expect questions along the lines of:

- 'Tell me about a time when you have had to use your initiative.'
- 'What do you understand by the phrase "using your initiative"?'
- 'How do you decide when it is appropriate to use your initiative and when you should refer a decision to your manager?'

'enjoy working to target'

aka: enthusiastic about exceeding targets, goal driven, results oriented

You'll most commonly find this in ads for sales positions. Not the kind of job where you answer the phone and take orders, but the kind where you actively go looking for sales. The whole idea is that you have a set number or value of sales to achieve each week or month. As soon as you look as if you can comfortably achieve it, up goes the target. Some people find this competitive approach extremely motivating – they're the people this employer is looking for.

Demonstrating it on paper

Obviously other related jobs are going to be important here. But you can highlight any kind of job where you've had to meet specific preset targets. Make sure you spell this out under responsibilities: *meeting monthly target for number of orders processed* or whatever.

Goal oriented hobbies also indicate the kind of personality which enjoys working towards targets. From rally driving to competitive bridge, make sure you mention anything which shows you're motivated by achieving a goal.

Demonstrating it face-to-face

The fact that this is mentioned at all in the ad indicates that it's an important part of the job. So you can expect to be asked questions about it. The interviewer will want to hear about the kind of target oriented jobs and activities you've found yourself attracted to in the past, and about how successfully you've met your targets.

Once you're in the interview, you have a goal – to get the job. Your interviewer knows this. So you need to be seen to be working enthusiastically towards this goal:

■ Sound keen and enthusiastic.

■ Give full answers to the questions, and volunteer relevant information.

■ Remember you're selling yourself to a customer – think of your interviewer as a buyer. This means listening carefully to them, as a good sales person would to a customer, and making sure you counter any objections they seem to have when they express doubts, such as: 'You don't seem to have had a great deal of sales experience,' or 'You've changed jobs rather frequently in the past, haven't you?'.

When your interviewer asks you if you have any questions of your own, ask intelligent questions which show you're focused on achievement. For example:

■ 'What opportunities are there to gain extra qualifications or experience?'

- 'Do you have any reservations about my ability to do this job?' (This is a classic sales person's question.)
- 'If I were offered this job, where would you see me in five years' time?'

'positive attitude'

aka: 'can-do' attitude

Some people are always negative. Give them a challenge and they'll list all the reasons why it can't be done and it's not worth trying. Others are always ready to look on the optimistic side and find ways that the thing *can* be done. Your attitude to a challenge largely determines whether or not you succeed. As Henry Ford said: 'Whether you believe you can, or whether you believe you can't, you're absolutely right.' (You can quote this in your interview.)

This employer wants to be sure you're one of the positive types. This is a job full of challenges, presumably, and they're looking for someone who believes they can overcome the obstacles and meet the challenges, and who will do it cheerfully and optimistically.

> **Hidden meaning**
>
> Although this is generally a legitimate and honest requirement, it can occasionally conceal the fact that this is a demoralizing job full of unattainable challenges. A positive attitude will help the employer, because it means you'll be less inclined to complain or to leave the job.
>
> **Key question**
>
> This is one of those issues that the interviewer isn't going to admit to. But you can probe in a way which will give you a more reliable idea of what kind of job you're letting yourself in for. Try asking: 'You mention that a positive attitude is important. What sort of challenges can I expect in this job?'

Demonstrating it on paper

It's not easy to demonstrate an attitude on paper, but if you can show yourself as the kind of person who invites challenges, that will imply that you enjoy them and are positive about them. So highlight your most challenging jobs, and make it clear what the challenges were.

Likewise, give examples of other activities, from voluntary work with the mentally ill to hang gliding. It all helps build a picture of you as someone with a positive attitude towards challenge.

Demonstrating it face-to-face

You'll need to arrive at the interview armed with examples of challenges you've faced and enjoyed. You should be ready to answer questions such as:

- 'What is your attitude when you're faced with a major challenge?' This is where you can quote Henry Ford.

- 'When have you failed to meet a challenge in the past, and why?' Pick an example a long time in the past, and show how you were positive about learning from your failure.

'able to work unsupervised'

aka: able to work with minimal supervision, ability to manage yourself

This phrase usually (though not always) applies to routine rather than project based jobs. When employers want someone to work alone on a project they tend to use the phrase 'self motivated' or 'highly motivated' (see page 123). The more low key phrase 'able to work unsupervised' generally implies that the work doesn't involve a great deal of decision making, but does call for self discipline and some initiative (see page 128).

To work productively when you're unsupervised you need to:

- Be disciplined about time keeping.
- Be able to resolve minor problems without help.
- Take basic decisions on your own initiative.
- Keep your motivation going without constant encouragement from above.

Demonstrating it on paper

Obviously it helps if you can show that you're used to working without a boss around, whether at home or in an office, or out on the road. It will also help if you can show that working unsupervised extends into your other activities. So if you've studied for an Open University degree, for example, this will count in your favour.

Demonstrating it face-to-face

As well as wanting to know about your past experiences, the interviewer is likely to ask you:

- 'What qualities you think you need to work effectively without supervision.'
- 'How you feel about working unsupervised.'

You can use the guidelines above, and think through for yourself what you believe are the important skills for working without a manager present. That way, you'll have a well prepared answer for your interviewer, which shows you've given the subject plenty of thought.

'quality approach to work'

Do you make a point of doing the job accurately and well, or just getting it done? No prizes for guessing which approach this employer is after. They're looking for someone thorough, who takes pride in delivering the highest possible standard.

This might sound obvious, but in fact there are employers out there who would rather you did the job fast, or kept the budget down. High quality work isn't always fast and it isn't necessarily cheap – even in terms of your own time if nothing else. So this employer is letting you know that quality is the top priority in this job.

Demonstrating it on paper

Your background – both at work and outside – will give clues as to how quality-oriented you are. If you're a model maker in your spare time this implies greater attention to quality than if you play paintball games at weekends. So think about what your hobbies say about you. And as far as work is concerned, flag up those jobs where quality has been a priority.

You need to make sure that your application is top quality. No spelling mistakes, crumpled paper, crossings out, poor layout. Your covering letter, CV and application should all reek of quality.

Demonstrating it face-to-face

This is one interview to turn up on time for, and with any paperwork you need at your fingertips, and all your preparation done. If you can't turn in a quality performance at interview, they'll never believe you can do it if they give you the job.

The interviewer will want to know about your attitude to turning in quality work:

- 'What jobs have you done in the past where quality was paramount?'
- 'What do you think are the essential ingredients of quality?'
- 'If you had to choose between turning in a job to a high standard but late, or on time but lower standard, which should you choose?' (The correct answer here is neither, by the way. You should avoid getting yourself into that position. If it's forced on you by circumstance, however, you should ask your boss for advice rather than deliver on time but compromise the quality.)

You need to give the clear impression that you have thought about these issues, and can answer these questions readily. If you've never thought about it, after all, how can you set such store by quality?

'disciplined'

aka: disciplined approach to work, well established work ethic

This is really all about getting on with the job properly rather than turning up late, not concentrating on your work, taking too many tea breaks, or chatting to your colleagues instead of focusing on the job.

The implication here, too, is that you need to apply this disciplined approach yourself: in other words there won't be a manager cracking the whip all the time. That's why the employer needs you to come complete with your own self-discipline.

Demonstrating it on paper

This is one of those requirements where a well presented application is even more important than usual. After all, if your application looks scrappy or is full of spelling mistakes, you're hardly likely to be a disciplined worker.

If you've had to apply self-discipline in the past, highlight it in your application and your CV. Specify that a certain job involved *being responsible for my own time keeping* or that it entailed *meeting preset workload targets each day* (you can't do that successfully if you're not disciplined).

Demonstrating it face-to-face

This interviewer is going to ask you to tell them about jobs which have entailed discipline in the past, so have your examples prepared. They may also ask you questions to find out more about your approach such as:

- 'If you sat next to a very chatty colleague who was always distracting you from your work, what would you do about it?'

'efficient'

Efficient people can be relied upon to get the job done. They always do what they say they will, take accurate messages with all the necessary details, remember everything they're supposed to, and keep other people on the ball too. They never miss an appointment or even a promised phone call, they deal with mail, email and phone messages promptly, and at the end of the day they've not only completed everything on their 'to do' list but they've tidied the desk and done all their filing as well.

Demonstrating it on paper

The best way to demonstrate your efficiency is by submitting a beautifully organized and presented application, with no mistakes or corrections. Send it in as promptly as you can.

When you're offered an interview, ask all the questions you need to in one call. Don't ring back two days later asking them to resend the directions because you've lost them.

Demonstrating it face-to-face

Turn up a few minutes early for the interview. If you're supposed to have brought any paperwork or portfolio material with you, make sure everything is to hand and you can find it all easily.

Your interviewer will judge your efficiency on appearances to some extent, but they will also ask you questions about how you schedule your time, and what systems you have for making sure you're efficient. This means 'to do' lists, a detailed diary, and various time management techniques such as dealing with all post as soon as it comes in, or clearing the day's filing each evening before you go home. So prepare answers to this kind of question, together with anecdotes about how you put these systems into practice.

'calm under pressure'

aka: able to work well under pressure

Whether the building has caught fire, a major deadline is looming or a customer is threatening to get your entire department sacked, it's always best to respond calmly. Not all of us can do it though. If you're one of those who is good at working under pressure, this could be the job for you.

Hidden meaning

The meaning here is barely hidden. Clearly this job entails a great deal of pressure. If it's a job in live television, or working in a shelter for homeless people, this is hardly surprising. But if you're applying to be an accounts manager or a landscape designer, you might question why this job should be so pressured that it's worth mentioning in the ad. Are they desperately understaffed? Is the management system hopelessly inefficient? It's worth identifying the source of the pressure to make sure you're happy to work with it.

> **Key question**
>
> Ask your interviewer: 'You mention that the job involves working under pressure. What kind of pressure is involved?'

Demonstrating it on paper

You need to highlight jobs you've done in the past where you had to work in a pressured environment, and say what your role was when things became stressed. If you were responsible for managing other people, or resolving problems, make this clear on your CV.

Demonstrating it face-to-face

This interviewer is going to ask you:

- About times you've been under pressure in the past and how you coped.
- About your strategy for handling crises.
- About how you would handle a particular situation which might arise in this job.

They may also deliberately put you under pressure to see how you respond. This might involve asking aggressive questions, such as: 'I can't see why you've applied for this job. You're underqualified.' Or they might ask in an aggressive manner or tell you to hurry up and answer quickly. Whatever technique they use, recognize that this is probably a test. Your response should be:

- Stay calm.

- Don't get defensive.

- Give yourself time to answer the question properly. Don't allow yourself to get flustered or be rushed.

'good problem solver'

aka: commercial approach to problem solving

There's a bottleneck in production, and you need to work out how to resolve it. Or maybe the new project is proving almost impossible to schedule – you need the prototype ready in four weeks but it's going to take six weeks minimum. Or perhaps Janet on the accounts desk insists on taking her full lunch break even though there's no one else who can cover.

In order to solve problems effectively you need to:

- Stay calm about the issue.
- Think analytically when necessary.
- Be creative in coming up with solutions and alternatives.

A commercial approach to problem solving essentially means that you can solve problems without costing the organization money. Solutions which blow the budget aren't really very helpful: this employer wants to be sure you can come up with cost effective solutions to problems.

> **Hidden meaning**
>
> What problems? Is this a job where you would expect to encounter challenging problems or not? If so, this is a genuine requirement. But if it surprises you that problem solving is specifically required, you need to find out more. It could be that this employer is inclined to set you impossible tasks, or perfectly possible tasks on impossible budgets or timescales. If so, they don't really want a problem solver at all but a miracle worker. The problem with this kind of job is that instead of being challenging it's simply demoralizing.
>
> *Key question*
>
> You need to know what you're dealing with, so ask. Tie the question into the ad: 'You say you're looking for a good problem solver. What sort of problems would I encounter?'

Demonstrating it on paper

As well as highlighting past experience of problem solving at work, you can also demonstrate that you enjoy tackling problems in other ways. Whether you are a crossword fiend or do voluntary work for the Citizens Advice Bureau, anything that shows you enjoy this kind of challenge will look reassuring on your CV.

There are different kinds of problems that you could encounter depending on the job, so think about what this employer is after, and pick out the most relevant skills and experiences in your application. For example, if it's a job as a project manager, you'd expect to encounter logistical problems. A park ranger would be more likely to come up against people related problems, while an engineer could expect technical problems.

Demonstrating it face-to-face

Problem solving may be an extremely important part of the job, and it's certainly important enough to feature in the ad. So you can expect plenty of questions. Prepare for questions such as:

- 'What is the trickiest problem you've encountered at work, and how did you deal with it?'
- 'What is your general strategy when you're faced with a difficult problem?'

Make sure you pick examples which relate to the kind of problem you'd expect to encounter in this job and, especially if this interviewer is after a commercial approach, try to find examples where you've saved money or minimized costs while solving the problem.

'relish a challenge'

Some of us like to know what we're doing, sticking to routines or tasks which we know we're good at. And some of us like doing something which we *think* we can do, but we've never tried. We enjoy the excitement and perhaps even the risk of a challenge. It can be scary, but the feeling of satisfaction when it's successfully completed makes it worthwhile.

Hidden meaning

Most employers asking for someone who likes a challenge are entirely genuine. They're looking for someone to take on a big project or task, and anyone who doesn't relish a challenge is going to be daunted and demoralized. This in itself can turn potential success into failure.

However, some employers are actually looking for someone to do the impossible. Maybe they don't realize themselves that it's impossible, but they must know it's a long shot. If you take this job, you'll soon become frustrated and fed up – for someone who enjoys a challenge there are few things more depressing than fail-ure. What's more, if the employer is in denial about the challenge being impossible, they'll blame you when the project fails.

Key question

There's no one specific question to resolve this. Essentially you're going to have to pick up a feel for how realistic the challenge is. Ask the interviewer to give you plenty of information about the project or task, and form your own opinion about whether it can be done. Keep asking until you have enough information.

You may feel that what you're being asked is possible but not in that time frame, or not on that budget, or only with more skilled staff. If this is the case, say so. Suppose you want the job, but only if the challenge can be met. In that case, tell the interviewer: 'I'd love to have a crack at this, and I know I can do it. My only reser-vation is that I don't believe it can be done properly in under six months. If the deadline were extended it would still be demanding but it would certainly be possible.'

You have nothing to lose with this approach. You look keen, you sound ready for the challenge, and you should be able to justify your reservations. This is enough to impress most interviewers. If the employer really won't budge, do you actually want to take on a doomed project? Wouldn't it be better if they gave it to someone else?

Demonstrating it on paper

Highlight plenty of examples of challenges you've taken on – and successfully met. From launching a new project to con-verting a barn, you want to show that you're the kind of person who goes through life looking for challenges.

Demonstrating it face-to-face

Your enthusiasm for challenges needs to come across. The interviewer wants to see that you're excited at the prospect of a stimulating project to get your teeth into, and that you don't contemplate failure. Once you take on a challenge, you meet it.

You'll need plenty of examples of challenges you've taken on in the past, and you'll need to give clear, quantifiable indications of your success. You can expect this interviewer to ask you questions about your approach to a challenge, such as:

- 'What is the biggest challenge you've ever taken on?'
- 'Have you ever failed to meet a challenge?'

'attention to detail'

aka: methodical

If your school reports all said *needs to avoid silly mistakes* (like mine did) this might not be the job for you. This is a job where detail is important – maybe it involves figurework, or proof reading, or running events where all the little things have to be taken care of.

You need to be the kind of person who checks and double checks, and thinks of everything, if you're going to impress this employer. It's likely that you'll know from the job itself what kind of details we're talking here: figures for an accounting job, organizational details for a PR assistant, and so on.

Demonstrating it on paper

The best demonstration, apart from past experience where attention to detail was vital, is a perfect application. Every 'i' dotted and every 't' crossed. That will spell out your credentials better than anything else, and will be enough at this stage to persuade the employer to shortlist you for interview.

If this is particularly important to the job, the employer might want to ask one of your referees about your attention to detail, so it's a good idea to give at least one referee who can vouch for it.

Demonstrating it face-to-face

It won't help if you go into the interview with your hair in a mess or your tie skew-wiff. As a matter of fact, some geniuses for detail are pretty sloppy dressers, but that's not the perception so you need to make an effort for this interview.

The interviewer will ask you questions about the kind of detailed work you've done before, and may ask you about how you make sure you don't miss anything. People who always get the detail right don't have any special skills or superhuman memories (as you'll know if you're one of them). What they have is a system. Maybe they write everything down, or perhaps they go through all the figures twice, or they check proofs once for spellings and then again for grammatical errors. Think about what your system is so you can impress your interviewer with a well thought out method to ensure that every detail is spot on.

'willingness to carry out duties'

This should be fairly self explanatory. This employer is probably fed up with staff who moan and complain, especially about the jobs no one much cares for whether it's filing or setting up the exhibition stand. This time round they want someone who is friendly (see page 96), co-operative and enthusiastic (see page 93).

Demonstrating it on paper

This isn't easy to demonstrate in your application – and the employer won't be expecting proof at this stage – but you can still give clues. You can mention in your covering letter that you're enthusiastic and enjoy work, and you can show in your CV that you've successfully done jobs which included quite a lot of uninteresting tasks.

Demonstrating it face-to-face

The best way to reassure your interviewer that you're a willing worker is to come across as enthusiastic and positive (see page 103). On top of that, be ready to give examples of tasks you've had to carry out in the past which didn't inspire you but which, nonetheless, you carried out happily. If you can, use these examples to illustrate other points you want to get across as well. So if the ad also calls for, say, efficiency, you can prepare an example where you've been efficient about the filing or purging the mailing list.

The interviewer may well ask you how you feel about doing tasks which you don't particularly enjoy – or even which you dislike. Obviously you should reassure them that you appreciate these tasks have to be done, and the best way is to do them quickly and efficiently. Since they have to be done, you might as well be cheerful about it, or you're the one who loses out.

'not a clock watcher'

It's pretty clear this employer doesn't want you working to rule. You need to be flexible enough (see page 121) to recognize that the job needs to be done, even if you miss part of your lunch break or go home a few minutes late.

The problem with clock watchers is not simply that the employer loses a few minutes of your time here and there. It's that your heart isn't really in the job if you're always thinking about how soon you can get away. They want someone who cares about the job, and that means being prepared to put in a little extra time when it's needed.

Hidden meaning

Unless you're looking for a job that will fill your long empty evenings for you, you need to make sure that this isn't the employer's way of making sure you don't complain when they overwork you and expect you to stay late every night clearing the ▶

backlog. It's one thing to put in occasional extra time when it's needed, and quite another to be exploited.

Key question

Unless the issue of hours is raised by the interviewer, this is a dodgy topic to tackle at the interview. As soon as you start asking at this stage, it will make you look like a clock watcher even if you're not. However, you don't actually need to know yet. Look out for clues, but don't raise the subject until you've been offered the job. Then ask what your hours will be – an entirely reasonable question at that stage.

Demonstrating it on paper

The best way to do this is when you list your responsibilities in past jobs. You can mention *working extra hours as necessary* to show that you're not a jobsworth when it comes to time keeping.

Demonstrating it face-to-face

Your interviewer may well ask you how you feel about working extra hours when the job calls for it. You need to answer along the lines that the important thing is to do the job effectively, and you recognize that sometimes this involves missing lunch or staying late when the pressure's on.

If you're concerned that this employer might expect more than you're prepared to give, you can preface this by saying something like: 'I have other commitments which mean I can't work late on a regular basis, but I can arrange it when I need to.'

'imaginative use of resources'

I like this one: it's an imaginative use of wording. It basically means that resources are limited, and you'll have to manage – and manage effectively – on what you've got. This might be a teaching post in a primary school where you'll need to be a dab hand with empty cereal packets and sticky backed plastic, or it may be a job as a hospital administrator where you have to juggle beds, staff and tight budgets.

Whatever the job, this employer wants you to do magic with the resources, and do it with good grace too. They've warned you before you've even applied for the post that you'll need to be 'imaginative', so they won't want any moaning about the budget once you're in post.

Hidden meaning

The only risk here – given that the employer has effectively put their cards on the table – is that the resources are so scarce that ►

> it's impossible to do anything useful with them no matter how imaginative you are.
>
> **Key question**
>
> You'll need to ask the interviewer for an example of the kind of problems they've encountered lately which have required an imaginative approach to resolve.

Demonstrating it on paper

Make sure you mention any relevant experience, and include any mention (in the responsibilities section) of jobs where you've had to *allocate resources on a tight budget*.

If the use of resources has a practical angle – such as a primary school teacher designing inexpensive projects, or a gardener reusing materials as pots and vegetable planters – give any examples you can of times you've practised these skills on a tight budget and what you've made.

Demonstrating it face-to-face

You're likely to be asked for past experiences of coming up with creative solutions on a tight budget. And try to think through the kind of problem you might realistically face in this job, because the interviewer may ask you a 'What would you do if. . .' question to test your imaginative talents.

You don't necessarily have to come up with an answer – you can simply show your approach. You might say: 'I'd consult the children. . .' or 'I'd consider alternatives such as using the private sector or top and tailing patients two to a bed. . .' (ok, maybe not that last one). The point is, you're not expected to know enough detail of the job to give a conclusive answer: the interviewer just wants to see how your mind works, and whether you can be creative about the kind of solution you come up with.

'ability to multi-task'

Can you juggle lots of different things at once? Can you, for example, organize a conference – book the venue, arrange the speakers, design and commission the invitations, plan the catering, check they have the right number of chairs, organize top management's travel and accommodation – and prepare a major report at the same time? Without letting the emails or the filing pile up?

Yes, it's one of those jobs where you have to keep dozens of balls in the air most of the time. Some people do it naturally – even work better that way – while others just crack up under the pressure. Multi-tasking (to use the jargon) is a valuable skill, and if you can do it well you could be the answer to this employer's prayers.

Demonstrating it on paper

If you're a natural multi-tasker, the chances are it will show on your CV. All you need to do is highlight the key points. Make sure you list the relevant tasks under 'responsibilities', and you can even use the term multi-tasking in your description, for example: *responsibilities included multi-tasking between conference organizing, research and office management.*

As far as activities outside work are concerned, play down any interest in competitive chess and flag up such things as stage managing the local dramatic society's plays. People who multi-task well tend to do it naturally whether they're at work or not.

Demonstrating it face-to-face

Have plenty of anecdotes prepared before you get to the interview, so you can readily describe times you've had to juggle numerous tasks. You need to sound as though you enjoyed it, even if it did get frenetic at times: good jugglers generally enjoy it even if they don't always admit to it.

The biggest risk with this kind of juggling is that balls will get dropped – things will be forgotten or done wrong. So your interviewer may ask you to describe how you prevent this from happening. Skilled multi-taskers use copious lists which they check through constantly: your interviewer will want to know that you have some kind of system so tell them how you do it.

'forward thinking'

This job is going to involve some kind of development – of a project or a department. It may even involve *launching* a new project or department. Such jobs need managers who can look ahead and think in the long term. What will be needed in two years, five years, ten years, and what can you do now to prepare for it?

You'll need to generate ideas – words such as 'innovative' (page 3) often appear alongside 'forward thinking' – and plan the budget well ahead. Some long term plans need to be initiated years ahead: forging partnerships, raising funds, getting planning permission and so on are all long range initiatives. Without forward planning now, they won't happen when the time comes.

Demonstrating it on paper

You need to show that you've worked on or set up long term projects in the past, preferably in some kind of management capacity (in other words you've been the one who had to do the forward planning). This might be a major project or new departure for the company, or it may be a smaller project but with a long term view. Spell out under 'responsibilities' the kind of long term considerations you had, for example *planning maintenance budget for next five years*.

Demonstrating it face-to-face

Spend some time before the interview thinking about what the long term considerations for this particular job are likely to be. Your interviewer will ask you questions about it, and this will give you a chance to show off your forward thinking skills and tell them what factors you would expect to plan ahead: budget, staffing, expansion or whatever.

You're bound to be asked about your past experience in forward planning, and you'll need examples which show that you are capable of thinking in the long term.

'independent'

aka: enjoy working independently

Whether you're working at home, in an office, on site or on the road, you won't have much company around. Some people love this: they enjoy being alone and find it far more productive. Other people go into decline when they're deprived of company for long periods. Neither is right nor wrong: it's just a matter of personality.

If you feel happier surrounded by other people, this may not be the job for you. If everything else seems perfect then go ahead and apply, but check this angle out carefully at interview before committing yourself if you get the job.

This can overlap with being 'able to work unsupervised' (page 136), and you may find both requirements in the same ad. However, they're not necessarily the same thing. Being independent is about working alone, whereas when you work unsupervised you may be surrounded by people, it's just that your boss won't be one of them.

Demonstrating it on paper

Highlight those jobs where you've had to spend time working alone. Even if it hasn't been full time, you may have worked from home two days a week, or gone out on site every Friday.

As well as work experience, your hobbies will say a lot about whether you really enjoy solo pursuits. So let the employer know if you enjoy reading, or are a keen walker or gardener. All of this helps build an image of someone who enjoys being alone.

Demonstrating it face-to-face

This isn't one of those complex skills the interviewer needs to probe in depth. They just need to be sure that you won't leave the job in three months' time because you're feeling miserable and isolated. So be ready to reassure them, with examples, that you're well used to being on your own, and let them know why it isn't a problem:

- You enjoy it (this is important).
- You find it far more productive (they'll like this, and it's certainly true).

The only word of warning is that you don't want to come across as anti-social or tricky and belligerent to work with. Let the interviewer know that you like other people's company, but you prefer to do focused work alone and then you can enjoy interacting at team meetings and so on.

V

CUSTOMER
RELATIONS

'positive approach to customer service'

aka: customer focused, focused on client service, customer aware

Clearly this is a job which involves spending time with customers. Some sales and customer care staff – I'm sure you've encountered plenty – are sullen and unco-operative. They couldn't care less whether you leave satisfied or not, just so long as they get to go home on time. If you get frustrated or angry, they will respond in kind. If you're on the phone to them and show your annoyance, they'll just hang up.

This employer wants to be sure you're not one of them. Whether you'll be dealing with customers constantly, or will be in a management role and only deal with them occasionally, they need to know that you will treat their customers politely and helpfully no matter how curt they are, and will go out of your way to make sure they have a good experience of the organization.

Hidden meaning

If all your customers are polite and straightforward, it's hard to handle them badly. Sure, the employer still wants you to be friendly and polite, but that's hardly worth flagging up with phrases like 'positive approach'. The chances are this is important to the employer because they know that quite a few of their customers can be tricky. Maybe you'll have to deal with complaints, difficult queries or angry customers.

Key question

Ask the employer: 'Will I be handling complaints?' or 'Are some of your customers stressed or upset before they reach the customer service desk/careline/customer care manager?'

Demonstrating it on paper

Your personable manner and helpful approach might be obvious when you meet someone, but you've got to get it across on your application form. Not so easy. Remember, however, that the application needs to be good enough only to get you the interview, where you can really prove yourself. You don't have to demonstrate an interpersonal skill like this absolutely on paper – that's really not possible. You just have to show enough promise of it for the employer to decide you're worth interviewing.

The kind of things which will tell the employer you can handle customers well are situations and jobs where you've had to deal with difficult customers, or other people. Anyone who puts themselves in line for handling difficult people must be reasonably good at it. So flag up:

- Any experience of complaint handling (mention it on your CV, for example: *Sales executive, JKL & Co – handling sales and customer queries, and dealing with problems and complaints*).

- Any jobs which clearly involve dealing patiently with demanding customers, such as working on the customer service desk at a mainline railway station, or working on a software support careline.

- Any non-work experience which shows that you're happy handling tricky people, such as voluntary work for Help the Aged or helping to run challenging outward bound courses.

Demonstrating it face-to-face

This is actually easier than showing this skill on paper. You obviously need to come across from the start as friendly and keen to impress – but then you should already be doing that for any interview.

If a positive approach to customer care (or whatever they like to call it) is high enough up this employer's list of priorities to be worth mentioning in the recruitment ad, they're going to ask you questions designed to find out if you've got it. So have your answers ready, and look for opportunities to tell the interviewer about times you've handled tricky customers effectively:

- Have two or three anecdotes prepared about times you've encountered angry customers, or difficult requests from customers. Choose examples which are varied, and which relate as closely as possible to the job you're applying for. So if this is a phone based job, make most of your examples about handling people on the phone.

- You'll have other anecdotes ready to demonstrate other requirements from this job ad (yes, you will), so try to choose some which also demonstrate your positive approach to customers. If you're demonstrating your honesty, for example, try to do it with an example of a time you've been honest in the face of a tricky customer and ended up leaving them impressed and happy.

'enjoy dealing with people'

Clearly this job is going to entail plenty of interaction with other people. If you're a loner who likes sitting in a corner getting on with your own self-contained work, this job ain't for you. In fact, this is going to be a job which doesn't simply involve working alongside other people, but which actively requires you to spend a lot of your working time dealing with them.

That word – 'dealing' – implies that the people in question need a certain amount of careful handling. It's not just cosy chatting, but time spent solving their problems, eliciting their co-operation or handling potentially tricky behaviour.

Hidden meaning

The writing between the lines in this job ad suggests that whoever these people are, they could be tricky to deal with. After all, most of us enjoy spending easy time with other people: that's hardly worth flagging up in an ad. What this employer may want you to ▶

enjoy is spending time being shouted at or verbally abused. Think about the kind of people you're likely to encounter in this particular job. Suppose the post being advertised is a client advisor in the local DSS office. The phrase 'must enjoy dealing with people' could mean you're going to have to cope with people whose applications for payments have just been refused.

Key question

Ask the interviewer something along the lines of: 'What's the general mood of most of your clients?' or 'Would I be dealing with difficult customers?'

Demonstrating it on paper

The best way to show in your application that you're a people person is to give plenty of examples of working with groups and teams of people, both in past jobs and outside work. If you've worked with difficult customers, do voluntary work for Help the Aged (for example), or organize motocross rallies in your spare time, put this in your CV and draw attention to it. You can do this by:

- Flagging it up briefly in the accompanying letter.
- Spelling it out in the CV by listing 'responsibilities included. . .' after the job or activity itself

Demonstrating it face-to-face

This is one of those qualities which your interviewer is going to judge largely by instinct. You need to come across as friendly and gregarious at interview, to *show* the interviewer that you enjoy dealing with people. Be ready to illustrate the examples in your CV with plenty of instances of the challenging people you've encountered and how you dealt with them.

It's possible that the interviewer may decide to test how you cope under pressure by becoming brusque or critical with you, maybe casting aspersions on your suitability for the job. Be prepared for this and show that you can handle it with grace and equanimity.

'excellent influencing skills'

aka: persuasive

This job is going to require you to talk people into doing things they didn't initially want to. Influencing people successfully largely stems from being able to put ideas to them in terms of benefits rather than features. This means not simply telling them what the result will be if they do as you suggest, but explaining what the benefit *to them* will be.

Suppose you want to persuade a customer to buy an umbrella. Don't just tell them the features: it's full size, black, with a wooden handle and it folds up. Point out how this benefits them: it's big enough to keep the rain off properly, it looks smart, it's really comfortable to carry, and when it's not raining you can simply store it out of the way in a bag.

Hidden meaning

Hmmm. Why are you going to need to be so good at influencing people? Presumably because you'll have to persuade people to do things they're reluctant to do. If this means persuading them to buy a product you know will help them but they just can't see it, that's fine. But would it have been worth mentioning in the job ad? Maybe so.

On the other hand, maybe it actually means persuading elderly people to go into a home when they really want to stay where they are. Or talking people with heavy debts into taking out a loan they can't afford. It may be well intentioned and honest, but it could still mean causing a lot of upset or encouraging people to make decisions you don't believe are right. Consider what the job being advertised is, and who you think you're likely to be expected to 'influence'.

Key question

Ask the interviewer: 'I notice you're looking for someone with "excellent influencing skills".Who would I need to influence, and why would they need persuading?' That should bring the facts out into the open.

Demonstrating it on paper

The key here is to express your CV in terms of benefits not features, to show you can think in those terms. So don't simply put down your relevant experience, but show how it benefits this employer. In other words, you don't simply write, for example:

- *June 2000 – September 2001: customer service manager at XYZ DIY store.*

Instead you put something like:

- *June 2000 – September 2001: customer service manager at XYZ DIY store.*

Responsibilities included dealing with customer complaints and problems. Plenty of experience calming down angry customers, resolving their problems and sending them away satisfied.

That's far more likely to convince this employer that you have what it takes.

Demonstrating it face-to-face

Your ability to influence the interviewer to offer you the job is going to be important here. Every time you persuade them that an unlikely looking qualification or experience is actually useful to this job, you demonstrate that you can influence people. So the entire interview is really an exercise in demonstrating this particular skill.

In addition to this, you obviously need to prepare examples of times when you've had to use all your powers of persuasion to get someone to do something. Make sure you select an instance where the person concerned came to realize that you had been right all along.

This is the kind of interview where the interviewer may throw out a sudden challenge, especially if it's customers you'll need to influence. Something like: 'Sell me this pen' or 'I hate holidays where you just sunbathe on beaches all day. Persuade me to go on holiday to Bermuda.' If this happens, just stay calm and think in terms of benefits, not features. Sell the pen, for example, by pointing out how impressive it looks, or how smoothly it writes, or how long it lasts. Or suggest that Bermuda is an ideal base for short-hop flights to the West Indies, New York, Florida and all sorts of interesting places with lots to do. You get the idea.

PART SIX

vi

MANAGEMENT

'good management skills'

This sounds as if it could mean practically anything, and it probably does. This employer is looking for a range of skills, all ones which good managers will possess. The sort of thing we're talking about here is:

- Being able to motivate people.
- The ability to recruit staff effectively.
- Good interviewing skills.
- Being able to organize a department and run it smoothly.
- Good budgeting skills.
- Good communication.
- Ability to run effective meetings.
- The ability to make good decisions and follow them through.

You won't necessarily be able to tell at this stage which of these is the most important to this employer. You may have to wait until the interview to find out which ones matter most (we'll come to that in a minute) but the job ad itself may give you some clues. For example, if it also lists 'good people skills' (page 75) or 'organizational skills' (page 215) this starts to give you a clue as to whether it's the people side or the systems side of management which is the top priority.

Hidden meaning

This requirement, more often than not, carries no worrying undertones in particular. However, occasionally it can be used to mask a particular area of management which is of special concern to the employer for a reason you might want to know about. For example, if the outgoing employee has left the department in an organizational shambles, or there's a real problem with staff retention, you want to find out. You'll probably get a good idea from the interviewer's line of questioning – they're likely to probe much more deeply into your experience of the particular aspect of management that concerns them.

Key question

If the interviewer seems overly concerned about one aspect of your management skills, for example dealing with people, try asking: 'Does this post involve dealing with challenging people?' This should elicit a useful response, and the word 'challenging' rather than 'difficult' implies that you're positive about such a prospect.

Demonstrating it on paper

Your application needs to flag up any management posts you've held, and you should list after each one, 'responsibilities included. . .' and then spell out the management skills you used in the job. In this way, you should be able to show that you have the experience this employer wants.

Don't forget that activities outside work can also say a great deal about you as a manager. Whether it's running a charity shop, organizing a youth club or managing your local cricket team, all these kinds of experience call for good management skills.

Demonstrating it face-to-face

This is your chance to find out what it is this interviewer is really after. When they ask you to talk about your management skills ask them: 'Is there any particular area of management that you particularly want to know about?' This will tell you whether you need to emphasize a specific area of your experience.

There's only one way to prepare for an interview which asks for good management skills. You need to come up with instances to demonstrate every one of the management skills the interviewer might want to know about. In fact, they may want to hear all of them. As well as examples and anecdotes, you also need to think through your approach to various management tasks so that you can express them coherently as though you know what you're doing and have an established procedure.

As far as your personal experiences are concerned, expect to be asked questions like:

- 'Tell me about a time when you've had trouble motivating someone, and what did you do about it?'
- 'Who was the most difficult employee you've ever had to cope with? How did you handle them?'

When it comes to procedures, have answers ready for questions such as:

- 'How do you make sure meetings run on time?'
- 'How do you go about recruiting a new team member?'

'skilled leader'

aka: ability to lead people, strong leadership ability, inspirational

This is all about motivation, really. Good leaders are, in essence, managers whose team members follow them willingly and enthusiastically. And they do that because the leader motivates them. So you've got to prove to this employer that you can inspire people to respect and follow you, and to do it because they want to.

If an employer bothers to mention this in the recruitment ad, it's because the team in question can only be successful with strong leadership. This is usually a close-knit group which works in a demanding field, often on project-based work, where they need to be deeply committed to each other and the project. Or, sometimes, the work involved is very challenging – maybe difficult, frustrating, or with long hours – so that a high level of motivation is necessary to keep the team members enthusiastic and committed to success.

Hidden meaning

There's not usually anything sinister in this requirement, but it can sometimes mean that the team in question is disparate or poorly motivated and needs bringing back into shape. You might relish the challenge of this, but even so you'd probably prefer to know if it's the case.

Key question

'How well motivated and bonded would you say the team in question is at the moment?'

Demonstrating it on paper

You have to demonstrate not only that you can manage a team, but also that you can inspire it. So you're going to have to identify times you've done this in the past, and find a way to highlight the fact in your application.

Any experience of successfully leading a project will help tremendously. The fact that the team succeeded indicates that it must have been well led. So your CV should:

- State the job in question.
- List 'responsibilities included. . .' and specify 'providing strong leadership', 'forming a well bonded team' or whatever relevant skill was the case for each of these.
- Outline the project and its outcome, for example: 'Project entailed planning and running major product launch at the NEC. Targets for promotion and subsequent sales were exceeded; budget was kept within target.'

Remember that team leadership outside work says as much about you as leadership at work does. So if you lead hiking trips in your spare time, or run charity events, this is all relevant information which you should flag up in your application.

Demonstrating it face-to-face

The universal image of a good leader is of someone dynamic and with a strong personality. In fact, some great leaders are quiet and retiring, but that's not unfortunately how the interviewer is likely to see it. They will be more impressed by your leadership qualities – rightly or wrongly – if you come across as a strong personality.

Now, there's no point trying to be something you're not. It never works, and if it did you could end up in a job that didn't actually suit you at all. But you can make sure that you project the most dynamic side of your genuine personality. Simply sounding decisive, avoiding lots of ums and ers, and speaking clearly without mumbling will help to spruce up your image as a natural leader.

Beyond your natural image and personality, you need to be ready to talk about your views on leadership and your experience of it. You might be asked, for example, to talk about what you think makes a good leader. Remember that the key is in motivation – creating a well bonded team and inspiring its members with the enthusiasm and energy to succeed.

When it comes to your experiences, be ready to talk about instances where you've provided strong leadership. What did you do to give your team that enthusiasm? Maybe you gave firm decisions, or perhaps you spurred them on after a failure so that their next project was a success. Or you might have taken the rap for them, or made sure senior management knew how well they'd done. Think of all the times you've done something to motivate your team rather than simply manage it, and be ready to give the interviewer these examples.

'ability to motivate people'

aka: ability to get the best out of people

If this employer is particularly concerned with your ability to motivate or lead the team as a whole, they're likely to ask for a 'skilled leader' or something of the sort (see page 188). When they specify that they want you to have the ability to motivate people, the chances are that they're concerned with motivating individuals.

Motivating people means, in the short term, getting them to approach their next task with enthusiasm every time. In the long term it means getting them to stay with the team and always give their best. Certain factors need to be present for people to be motivated:

■ They need to understand how their job fits into the organization, and therefore why they matter.

■ They need clear and achievable targets so they know what they're supposed to be doing and they can do it.

■ They need to feel involved in the job and the team – included in discussions, kept informed, and allowed to contribute to any decision making process.

It's your job as a manager to make sure that these factors are in place.

On top of this, everyone is motivated by other factors which vary from person to person – it might be money, status, responsibility, recognition, challenge, job satisfaction, security or something else. So it is also your job to find out what motivates each individual on your team, and make sure you provide that motivation. You cannot do this successfully unless you recognize that you need to treat each team member individually: one size doesn't fit all.

Hidden meaning

The concern here is that you might find, if you get this job, that you're in charge of several people – maybe even a whole team of them – who are badly demotivated and unco-operative at the moment. This is a challenge you might well relish. . .but then again you might not. So it's best to know.

Key question

'How well motivated would you say the team members in question are at the moment?'

Demonstrating it on paper

Tricky one this. But of course you have only to demonstrate enough promise on paper to get an interview. It's impossible to prove conclusively that you are a good motivator, but you can show that you've done jobs in the past that required you to motivate people, and if possible that you've been promoted or rewarded in some way that demonstrates that you did a good job of it.

So highlight those jobs you've done which involved getting the best out of people, and list the responsibilities involved, mentioning 'motivating team members' or 'taking on a demoralized team and motivating it' or whatever was the case.

After 'responsibilities' add also 'achievements' and list any concrete successes you and your team scored. However, these must be demonstrable – it's no good saying 'successfully motivated team members'. After all, you would say that, wouldn't you? You need to come up with something which shows that the team members must have been motivated: 'all original team members were promoted during my three years in the job' or 'unco-operative team member on final warning won departmental employee of the year award within twelve months' or 'departmental results increased by 300 per cent during my time as manager'.

Demonstrating it face-to-face

Ok, you've got an interview. Well done. Now you've got a chance to show that you really do know how to motivate people. Arm yourself with lots of instances of times you've successfully motivated people even when they've initially been uninterested or unwilling. If this interviewer is looking for the ability to motivate, they're bound to ask you lots of questions about this.

You also need to think through your ideas about motivation: what are the key ingredients of good motivation in your view, what motivates people in general, and so on. You can take the comments about motivation above, and also add your own views, to have answers ready to questions such as:

- 'How important do you think motivation skills are in a manager?'
- 'How do you get the best from people?'
- 'If you had to identify just one essential skill for motivating people, what would it be, and why? What about the top three skills?'

All these questions (and your interviewer may come up with many more like them) will call for examples from your own experience. But they also require you to have given some thought to the issue of motivation: what it is, why it matters and how it's done. Your interviewer will want to see that you're the kind of person who goes through this analytical and questioning thought process, so your answers need to appear well thought out, rather than off the top of your head. So don't start: 'Well, let me see. . .' but rather, 'It's an interesting question, and one I've thought about a lot. I've come to the conclusion that. . .' Now, doesn't that sound better?

'ability to develop a team'

aka: good team building skills

A team is more than simply a group of people working together. It is an almost living entity whose whole is greater than the sum of its parts. A team can do things that none of its individual members alone can do. And what really separates a good team from a mere collection of people is its attitude. A good team consists of members who are committed to the team as a whole and feel a strong identity with it. It should feel like a family of sorts.

A good team is better motivated than a group of workers, with lower staff turnover and higher productivity. There is more job satisfaction for the team members and problems are resolved much more smoothly and easily. So no wonder this employer wants you to be a team builder. Some of the skills you need to develop a strong team are hard to define, but they certainly include:

- Strong leadership (see page 188).
- Recruiting staff whose skills and natural abilities complement one another.

- Treating everyone in the team as an important part of it, from secretaries to project leaders.

- Bringing the team together as a whole frequently, for briefings, training and so on.

- Rewarding the whole team collectively for team achievements.

- Encouraging team members to support one another.

- Encouraging flexibility within the team, including putting different people in charge of different projects – this helps everyone realize that people are in charge of tasks, not in charge of each other.

The word 'develop' in the wording of this ad implies that this employer doesn't simply want you to be able to run a strong team, but to build one up in the first instance. This is likely to entail introducing many of the practices listed here, and perhaps recruiting or reorganizing staff to create an effective team.

Hidden meaning

The most likely unspoken scenario here is that the employer is looking for someone to lead a group of people who have been badly managed until now, and don't pull together as a team. They may also be poorly motivated individually. This is one of those hidden meanings which may actually conceal a challenge you would relish – think what turning round a team like this would do for your career; nevertheless, it's better if you can get this kind of information out in the open where you can consider it properly.

Key question

'Would you describe this group of people as a strong team at the moment?' If not: 'In what way do they need developing to make them a successful team?' A word of warning here. A good interviewer will give you a straight answer to a question like this: they need motivating, they need a project they can get their teeth into, the team needs balancing in terms of personalities, or whatever.

Some interviewers, however, answer this kind of question with a comment such as: 'That would be your job to work out.' In fact, if you get the job it's not your role to work out what's wrong – it's your job to put it right. If your employer doesn't even know what's wrong, or does but won't tell you, the chances are they're not going to be much more helpful once you're in post. An employer isn't there to set traps and tests for their managers: they're there to give all the help and support they can. So beware of this kind of interviewer, especially if they would become your line manager. If you take the job you could be in for a deeply frustrating time of it.

Demonstrating it on paper

Flag up all the instances you can of having developed a team during your career. Spell out what it entailed (under 'responsibilities included. . .') and how successful it was (under 'achievements').

Don't forget that building a team in activities outside work can be just as important as your work experience. If you've set up and organized an annual village fete, or built the local underwater hockey team up into a regional finalist, that's worth telling this employer about.

Demonstrating it face-to-face

This is simply a matter of having all your instances and examples ready: plenty of anecdotes to demonstrate your experience in building a team. Think about all the skills involved – use the list above to help you – and try to find an example of each from your own experience.

If you haven't had the opportunity to put some of these skills into practice, and therefore have no example to give, your next best bet is to quote someone else as an example. 'I've never needed to do it myself, but I do remember a boss of mine who was particularly good at it. She used to. . .' and so on. The point of this is that even though you haven't used the skill yourself, it shows that you recognize it, you've noticed when it has been used around you, and you've learnt from it. Finish up the anecdote by saying something like: 'I've always remembered that as a great example of pulling a team together, and it's certainly something I'd do myself in that situation.'

Team building is one of those skills which your interviewer will want you to have thought about. So as well as giving your own personal experiences, be prepared to answer questions along the lines of:

- 'How would you define a team?'
- 'What do you consider are the key ingredients that define a successful team?'
- 'Which skills do you think are the most essential to build a strong team?'

'ability to develop people'

This is really a question about training. Not necessarily running formal training courses, but training someone up by various means so that they become more valuable to the organization and to themselves. Someone who could once only answer the phone and do basic filing, for example, is eventually able to run a department, operate sophisticated computer programs, or give polished presentations. We've all been there – what we can do now is vastly more than we could when we started our first job. This employer wants to know that you can make it happen for your team members.

Developing people effectively entails:

- Identifying what skills they would like to learn, and also those which it would be useful for them to learn. These often overlap.

- Putting together an effective programme to help them learn. This involves setting (and adhering to) a timetable, and deciding on the best method of training: internal courses, external seminars, one-to-one training, evening classes, hands-on experience, group training and so on.

- Supporting them, monitoring their progress and providing additional help or experience when they need it.

- Giving them a chance to use their new skills once they have acquired them, both to keep them motivated and to get the best out of them.

Demonstrating it on paper

State any jobs you've done in which you had to develop people, including listing the relevant responsibilities. You also need to indicate any experience you have of training people, whether you've run courses or simply had someone sit beside you and learn from you. All this experience is relevant.

Demonstrating it face-to-face

As always, have plenty of examples ready to give your interviewer. One of the important things here is that many people equate developing people with training them, and therefore focus entirely on their experience of delivering training in various forms. People who think like this often give their teams haphazard training – maybe sending them on a course on a whim because it's there and looks as if it might be useful, rather than giving them a structured programme to follow.

You are likely to put yourself one up on most of your fellow candidates if you make it clear that you recognize the importance of:

- Taking the employee's personal career aims into consideration.

- Developing a plan for them.

- Setting a timetable and making sure it's followed.

- Monitoring their progress regularly.

- Providing support and back-up if they need it.

You should also expect to answer questions about the principles of training and developing people. So anticipate questions along the lines of:

- 'Why do you think developing people is important?' (Remember to think of it from the point of view of the employee's motivation and job satisfaction as well as from the organization's perspective.)

- 'What kind of training do you think is most effective?' (This is a trick question, really: the answer is that a mix is usually best, and that the choice should be adapted to the needs of the person concerned.)

'able to manage change'

aka: able to initiate change

Initiating and managing change aren't exactly the same thing, of course, but they tend to go hand in hand. Some people enjoy change while others resist it. If you're in charge of a team of people in a department which needs to change in terms of working patterns, procedures, staffing or location, for example, you'll need to enjoy change.

On top of enjoying it, you'll also need to be able to:

- Identify what changes need to be made.
- Project manage the process of changing.
- Persuade your team to accept the changes, especially those members who are reluctant to give up the status quo.

Demonstrating it on paper

You need to let this employer know that you've coped with change before, and coped well. Ideally, you need to have managed the process before, but if the rest of your credentials look good the employer might be prepared to take on someone with less experience of managing change.

While no one wants to employ a hardened job-hopper, this employer won't want someone who has been in the same job for several years (unless it involved managing a lot of changes). So include every job you've done – including any brief fill-in jobs – to show that you're not a stick-in-the-mud.

Set out in your CV any changes your past employers have been through which have affected you, such as *My time with ABC company saw them change from a regional based organization to a centralized one with branch offices*. Spell out changes to your own job, your department and the whole organization, and make it clear if you had any management role to play during the changes.

If you have any strong experience of change outside work, such as being brought up in an army family and changing schools nine times, this is also well worth highlighting as it shows you are naturally adapted to cope well with change.

Demonstrating it face-to-face

Your interviewer is going to ask you about the changes you've experienced in the past, how you've dealt with them, how much difference they've made and so on, so have answers ready to this kind of question.

They are also likely to ask you what are the key stages in managing change, and how you've managed the process in the past.

'able to manage the needs of shareholders'

Whoever owns the business you're applying to wants to see it grow as effectively as possible. For you to contribute to this, you need to look at the business as a whole, rather than at your section or department only. And you need to be able to balance your department's needs against those of the whole business. This requires a broad view and an understanding of the industry trends and economic factors which affect the business.

Hidden meaning

If you give to somewhere, you have to take from somewhere else. Stakeholders want the maximum profit, and to give it to them you have to minimize expenditure. This can mean cutting back on budgets for areas such as staffing, and you may not feel comfortable with this. Every company keeps staff costs at a sensible level, but not everyone has the same view on what constitutes a fair wage. You want to be sure that this isn't an employer who will ▶

---

expect you to compromise your principles in order to line shareholders' pockets.

Key question

Ask the interviewer about the kind of returns that shareholders
are looking for, and how tough you have to be to achieve these.

Demonstrating it on paper

Let this employer see evidence that you've been responsible in
the past for looking beyond your own department or team.
Detail other posts where your responsibilities have included
contributing to overall corporate strategy, or writing reports
which take the broader view into consideration.

Phone up and ask for a copy of the annual report (and study
it, of course). The fact that you've asked for it will look good.
Check out the website too.

Demonstrating it face-to-face

As well as furnishing yourself with examples of your experience of looking after shareholders, make sure you've done
your homework well, because this interviewer is going to ask
you about the company's overall concerns. You can expect
questions such as:

- 'What conflicts do you see between the needs of shareholders and the needs of employees, and how should you
  balance them?'
- 'What do you know about our company?'
- 'What do you think the key trends in the industry are?'

'able to develop the future strategy of the business'

aka: vision

Clearly you are going to be expected to contribute to the overall direction of the company if you get this job. You'll need to look beyond current concerns and judge what the overall trends in the industry are and how the organization can respond to them most effectively. This requires marketing skills in the broadest sense – from product development onwards – to assess how the organization fits into the market and how it can succeed in it.

Vision implies that not only can you see ahead and respond well in advance, but that you can also be pro-active, setting the trend yourself and seeing how the business will look in several years' time.

Demonstrating it on paper

The more experience you have of this in the past, the better. So make sure you highlight it in your CV and application. Anything which shows you've been involved at a level higher up than your own department – writing proposals or reports to the board, for example – will help. You also want to flag up any experience of planning well ahead, even if this has been only at departmental level (see also 'forward planning' page 164).

Demonstrating it face-to-face

The interviewer is bound to ask you about your experience in strategic thinking, both at section level and for the business as a whole. So prepare your examples and be ready to talk about what your contribution has been.

They will also ask you questions to test out your strategic thinking credentials, so be ready to answer questions such as:

- 'What do you see as the key trends in this industry?'
- 'What are the main factors we should consider when planning for growth?'
- 'How would you develop a vision for this business?'

When it's time to ask questions of your own at the end of the interview, ask some which show you naturally think in terms of organizational strategy. For example: 'Where do you see the organization in five years' time?'

PART SEVEN

vii

GENERAL SKILLS

'good analytical skills'

aka: analytical

The nature of the job itself will give you clues as to what you'll be expected to analyze – it could be figures or it might be technical. You'll need some experience – this isn't the kind of thing the employer is going to take on trust. It's likely to be central to the job if it's getting a mention in the recruitment ad, so you'll have to make sure this employer recognizes that you have a track record in analytical work.

Demonstrating it on paper

You can go right back to your school career if you're no more than a few years out of education. If you were choosing options such as chemistry and maths back then, it's a good sign that you're a naturally analytical kind of person. So highlight any school choices and good results in analytical subjects. Something less technical like history can also be highly analytical, and if you're applying for a job as, say, a researcher this would be an excellent background.

Make sure you flag up all the analytical tasks you've had to do in past jobs, as well as focusing on positions where the entire job was analytical. If this job appeals to you, the chances are it's because you have an analytical mind and your past choices will show this. It's just a matter of identifying the most persuasive examples and bringing them out.

This employer is probably going to consider evidence of analytical skills essential for shortlisting candidates for interview, so make sure you spell them out in your CV, and mention them in your covering letter too.

Demonstrating it face-to-face

Have all your examples and anecdotes well prepared for this interview. Your interviewer is bound to ask you for lots of evidence of your analytical abilities. You want to show that you're a naturally analytical thinker, and generally drawn to jobs which require this kind of approach.

Your interviewer will also want to see how you *feel* about this kind of work. If you're a natural at it, you'll also enjoy it, so they'll be looking for a sense that you relish this sort of mental challenge. If you don't actually enjoy it, you won't enjoy the job, so they need to be sure you'll be happy in the post if they offer it to you.

'organizational skills'

aka: systematic, logical, able to plan ahead

Some of us can organize anything, and some of us can't organize our way out of bed in the morning. This job might entail anything from organizing PR events or running a project to administering a busy office. But if you're a natural organizer it won't much matter – you could organize any of them.

This employer will want to know that:

- You can institute logical systems which everyone can follow.
- You can schedule projects.
- You can plan ahead.
- You can organize your time effectively.
- You can organize other people without putting their backs up.
- You can manage the details without letting them get forgotten (see page 153).

Demonstrating it on paper

As well as highlighting all your past experience of organizational tasks, you can also show that you enjoy organizing things outside work. Whether it's your best friend's wedding or the boy scouts' summer camp, it all shows that you enjoy organizing things.

On top of that, you'll need to organize your CV extremely clearly. This isn't difficult – you ought to be doing it anyway – but a badly organized CV is just about guaranteed to lose you this job. You won't even get an interview. Equally, you don't want to be phoning up every five minutes asking for more information, or directions to the interview. Wait until you have a list of everything you need to know, and then call once.

Demonstrating it face-to-face

Obviously you need to turn up on time to the interview, and with any paperwork readily to hand. The interviewer will ask you for evidence of your organizational skills, so be ready with your examples. In addition, you may be asked questions along the lines of:

- 'What systems do you use for staying on top of things?'
- 'Tell me about the most daunting organizational job you've ever done.'
- 'What's the worst mistake you've ever made when you've been organizing an event?' A tip here: make it totally understandable, relatively minor, and a long time ago – the implication being that you'd never do anything like that now. If you can, make it something non work-related too. And show how you've learnt from it so it can't recur.

'able to demonstrate accuracy'

This is similar to 'attentive to detail' (page 153) but there's an implication that this job involves figures or technical work where precision is called for. It might be accountancy or technical drawing – the kind of thing where a mistake leads to an overcharged (and angry) customer, or a window which doesn't fit in the space that's been left for it.

Demonstrating it on paper

Show the employer that you're the kind of person who enjoys precision work and is well used to it. From good results at A level science to examples of jobs where you've been trusted with important work which required accuracy, it all needs to be highlighted.

The kind of hobbies which call for accuracy also show you have a bent for this kind of thing – whether you're treasurer for a local society or you build Airfix models in your spare time.

Oh, and no spelling mistakes in your application.

Demonstrating it face-to-face

Expect to be asked about past work which has required accuracy, and about your methods for ensuring accuracy. Bear in mind that the fact you've been an accounts clerk, for example, doesn't prove you're accurate. You might have been a dreadful accounts clerk. The interviewer wants evidence to show that you did the job well – specific successes, promotions and so on. Or a time when your eye for accuracy picked up a vital mistake everyone else had missed.

Be prepared for the fact that the employer might ask you to take some kind of test. If this is more than a quick test, they should warn you in advance, but it never hurts to be prepared anyway. If you're expecting it, you're less likely to be thrown or panicked by it if it happens.

If you're given any kind of written paper, stay calm and always read through the whole paper before you begin. (Very occasionally sneaky employers will set a paper which contains some kind of trick question which you will spot too late unless you read the whole thing through before you start.) Remember, you're being tested for ability and accuracy, not speed, so unless the employer tells you you're competing against the clock, take your time. Double check all your answers, and check them once through again at the end.

'able to demonstrate numeracy'

You might well find this requirement in an ad for something like a warehouse manager. The job isn't centred around figurework, but if you aren't confidently numerate you won't be able to do the job well.

This is one of those skills which the employer needs to be sure you have, but once they're reassured they'll move on to the next thing. They won't focus on this because it's not the key to the job – you don't need to be a mathematical whizz – you just have to reach a minimum standard.

Demonstrating it on paper

You may be able to clinch this one easily. A good GCSE grade in Maths, or a past job calling for numeracy in which you got promoted, will put the employer's mind at rest. If you don't have any credentials of this kind, you'll need to find other ways to show you can reach the numeracy standard they're after.

Maybe you've worked in a shop or behind a bar; perhaps you've worked as a croupier for a charity casino, or maybe you play Scrabble of an evening. All of these things are impossible without basic numeracy skills. In fact, if you are numerate enough for this job, you're bound to have done something somewhere which has used your skills.

Make sure your application looks good. An illiterate application implies your numeracy skills may be as poor. Whereas a professional application (see page 27) implies good numeracy too.

Demonstrating it face-to-face

You may well be set a basic test here. Approach it calmly and don't rush. It's not a speed test, it's a numeracy test. Think through each question carefully to make sure you understand it, and that there's no catch to it. Check your answers thoroughly.

The interviewer will also ask you questions about past jobs where you've needed to be numerate, so prepare examples to give them.

'good IT skills'

aka: passion for technology

When you phone up to ask for an application for this job, ask them at the same time exactly what IT skills they want. On top of the specific requirements, they will also want to know that you have an ability to pick up new IT skills quickly. This is obviously a job where you need to be computer literate and able to upgrade your skills easily.

Demonstrating it on paper

The more computer experience you have, and the wider it is, the more confident this employer will feel with your application. So spell out your IT experience for each job (under 'responsibilities') but add another section to your CV headed 'IT skills' and list under it all the programs you're familiar with, all the training you've had, any qualifications and so on.

Demonstrating it face-to-face

Before you go to the interview, mug up on all the IT skills and programs you may be rusty on. If you can, find friends or colleagues who are using programs you've half forgotten and ask for a quick refresher course. This applies especially, of course, to any skills you've ascertained will be needed for this job. That way, you'll be able to answer any questions the interviewer fires at you to test your knowledge of particular systems.

You'll need to transmit a feeling that you enjoy working in IT, and you want to learn new skills. As you know, this is an area where technology moves fast, and you can't work in the field effectively without upgrading your skills regularly. So let the interviewer see that this is a prospect you relish. When they ask you for your own questions, you can ask them what new IT skills you'd get the chance to learn with the company. This will impress them with the fact that you're keen to increase your value to the organization, and that you really enjoy acquiring new skills.

'excellent administration skills'

Administration skills and organizational skills (see page 215) can be the same thing, and you may find them both listed in the same job ad. But administration skills specifically refer to routine work, rather than projects and events. To be a good administrator you need to set up effective systems, and to see that they are followed by everyone. You also need to stay on top of all the general paperwork, post, messages and so on.

Demonstrating it on paper

You'll need to highlight all the past jobs you've done where you had to administer a system or a department. Make sure you spell out under 'responsibilities' what administration was involved – don't assume it's obvious to the employer reading your application.

Demonstrating it face-to-face

The interviewer will want to know about your past experiences, so think through plenty of examples. As well as times
when you've run existing systems, give examples of systems
you've devised and set up yourself.

'strong financial awareness'

aka: commercially aware

Similar to numeracy (see page 219), this implies that you should also have a sense of the value of money. In other words, you won't waste it. You'll see this requirement in ads for jobs such as head chef, where working out costings and keeping within budget are essential.

Demonstrating it on paper

If you've held the same or similar kind of job before, you'll probably have had to be financially aware, so you can flag this up in your application. Also make sure you highlight any occasions you've been responsible for budgets, and if you've successfully stayed within them, say so.

Remember that experience outside work can say just as much about you as professional experience. If you've been responsible for buying in props and costumes for a school play, or keeping a Girl Guides' camping trip within budget, then say so.

Demonstrating it face-to-face

Obviously you need to arrive equipped with examples to give your interviewer of times you've kept costs down and stayed within budget. Make sure your answers to all other questions also reflect your awareness of the company's finances. Suppose you're applying for the job of chef and you're asked about how you'd be creative in the kitchen. Make sure you refer to staying within budget so the interviewer realizes that your financial antennae are permanently switched on.

'able to prioritize workload'

How do you cope when you seem to have more work than time? Which bits get done and which don't? The only effective way to deal with a large workload is to be canny about how you prioritize.

Ideally you need a system which involves:

- Listing the tasks which need to be done.
- Identifying which are the most important.
- Allocating them letters or numbers (1,2,3 or A,B,C) according to their importance.
- Marking urgent tasks (which may or may not be important) clearly and dealing with them first.
- Identifying and discarding tasks which don't need to be done at all – binning them, delegating them or passing them on.
- Working through the remaining tasks in order of importance.

This means that everything gets done eventually, and in order of importance, and the urgent tasks get dealt with promptly. This is one aspect of time management (see page 233).

Hidden meaning

No one has to prioritize a light workload – you can clear your desk every day. No, you'll need to prioritize in this job because the workload is heavy. If you're good at prioritizing this may not be a problem, or it may be only sporadically heavy and you can catch up in between. However, if it's too heavy for anyone to cope with it may be extremely demoralizing. So make sure this job isn't really two people's jobs rolled into one.

Key question

It's easy enough to ask straight questions here: 'How heavy is the workload? Is it always heavy or does it fluctuate?'

Demonstrating it on paper

Make it clear which jobs have involved dealing with a heavy workload, and include *prioritizing workload* under responsibilities.

Demonstrating it face-to-face

As well as giving plenty of examples of times you've had to prioritize your work, you can also expect to be asked questions about:

■ What system you use to prioritize.

- How you decide which tasks are most important. The answer is that the most important ones are those which most closely meet the objective of your job. If you're a marketing manager, for example, the most important tasks are those which actively help market the business. At the bottom of the list would come paperwork and administrative tasks (but these still need to get done).

'able to work to tight deadlines'

There are some jobs in which a missed deadline is a catastrophe. If you're in PR, for example, there's no point planning a major product launch if you can't get the product to the venue until two days after all your invited guests have been and gone. If you're a researcher, there might be dozens of people expecting your report on a particular day, with time set aside and meetings planned to deal with it.

Working to tight deadlines involves several skills:

- Being able to work well under pressure (see page 144).
- Effective time management (see page 233).
- Good organizational skills (see page 215).
- A disciplined approach (see page 140).

This employer will want to see evidence that you can do all these things in order to feel confident in your ability to meet deadlines.

> ## Hidden meaning
>
> Why are the deadlines so tight? Is it the nature of the job, or is this particular organization badly managed? If it's that kind of job, the tight deadlines are probably one of the reasons you want to apply – presumably you enjoy working in a high-pressure atmosphere. But if this isn't a job you'd expect to involve tight deadlines, you might want to know more. After all, working in a poorly managed system is demoralizing even if you do enjoy working to tight deadlines in principle.
>
> ### Key question
>
> Simply ask your interviewer: 'What kind of deadlines are involved? Why are they so tight?'

Demonstrating it on paper

The most convincing thing you can do is show the employer that you're already used to working to tight deadlines. So highlight all the jobs you've done in which you've had to do it. This might be central to the whole job, or it might simply be one part of it which you can list under 'responsibilities', for example *producing weekly figures by 3pm deadline every Friday* (it helps to get the word deadline in there, just so the employer doesn't miss the fact).

Remember that plenty of activities outside work also show you can work to deadlines. Organizing any kind of event, for a local society or charity, and of course any kind of theatre work such as stage managing the local operatic society performances.

Demonstrating it face-to-face

Collect together a mental list of all the times you've worked to tight deadlines which you can quote if called on. You may also be asked:

- 'What are the key skills you need to work to a deadline?'

- 'Have you ever missed a deadline, and what happened?' The answer to this should be no, although you mustn't lie about anything work related (if you have missed a deadline, see below).

- 'Tell me about the closest you've ever come to missing a deadline.' Pick something a fairly long time ago, and make sure the reason you nearly missed it was absolutely not your fault. Don't blame anyone else though – choose something which was caused by an act of God or a train strike or something of the sort. If you possibly can, also choose an example where the only reason you *didn't* miss the deadline was because of some smart work on your part.

'effective time manager'

Some people look immensely busy but never seem to get anything done, while others calmly and effectively work their way through a massive workload and get everything done on time.

A good time manager:

- Is disciplined (see page 140).
- Has good organizational skills (see page 215).
- Can prioritize their workload (see page 227).

On top of this, they simply don't waste a minute of their time. They group tasks together for maximum time efficiency, dealing with phone calls in batches, and emails twice a day instead of dotted throughout. And they can do two things at once: filing while holding on the phone, or catching up on reading while travelling (not while driving of course – except on the M25 at rush hour).

Diary skills are also important. Not only should appointments be listed in the diary, but also phone calls, notes to chase people up, and time set aside for working on projects. And all logged well in advance.

Demonstrating it on paper

Spell out all the jobs you've had which have called for effective time management, and list any particular requirements under 'responsibilities' such as *prioritizing a heavy workload*.

Don't submit this application at the last minute: it won't look good.

Demonstrating it face-to-face

You can expect this interviewer to question you about what time management techniques you use, to ensure that you really do know your time management skills. So be prepared to answer questions about:

- Diary keeping.
- Prioritizing.
- Techniques for using your time efficiently.

index